Wiza

anasoff

Their

Wizar
Wor

rds

and

rders

Fer

W

Howard

rd

Wizards and Their Wonders

Photographs by Louis Fabian Bachrach

By Christopher Morgan

Portraits in Computing

 ACM

 the **computer** museum

Library of Congress Cataloging-in-Publication Data
Morgan, Christopher (Christopher Patrick), 1949-
Wizards and their wonders: portraits in computing/by
Christopher Morgan: Photographs by Louis Fabian Bachrach.
    p. cm.
On t.p.: The Association for Computing Machinery and
The Computer Museum.
Includes biographical references and index.
ISBN 0-89791-960-2 (alk. paper)
1. Computer science – Biography. 2. Computer industry – United States – History.
I. Bachrach, Louis Fabian, 1950-. II. Association for Computing Machinery.
III. Computer Museum (Marlborough, Mass.) IV. Title.
QA76.2.A2M67 1997
004'. 092'2 – dc21
[B]   97-33234
                                                 CIP

Book design by Gill Fishman Associates/Cambridge

ACM Order Number: 710971

Additional copies may be ordered prepaid from:
ACM Order Department
P.O. Box 12114
Church Street Station
New York, NY 10257

Phone: 1-800-342-6626
(US and Canada)
+1-212-626-0500
(all other countries)
Fax: +1-212-944-1318
E-mail: acmpubs@acm.org
URL: http://www.acm.org

For Gwen — C.M. & L.F.B.

Preface

Wizards and Their Wonders: Portraits in Computing is a tribute by The Computer Museum and the Association for Computing Machinery to the many people who made the computer come alive in this century. It is unabashedly American in slant. The people on the list were either born in the United States or have done their major work there. With the exception of the Forerunners listed in the first section, the book concentrates on living innovators in computing, comprising: the Inventors, who created the work; the Entrepreneurs, who drove the work; the Communicators, who shaped the work; and the Venture Capitalists, who funded the work.

Wizards and Their Wonders was born when The Computer Museum's Founding President, Gwen Bell, and photographer Louis Fabian (Chip) Bachrach decided to create a personal photographic celebration of America's computer innovators as seen through Mr. Bachrach's eyes. He spent much of the following year photographing the people you see in this book, logging many miles in the process. All the photographs, with the exception of the historical photographs in the Forerunners chapter, are his work. **They offer a unique record of one of the most extraordinary groups of innovators in the history of technology.**

Why the emphasis on America? Quite simply, the latter half of the twentieth century in America has offered a unique incubator to support the development of the computer. America's post-World War II economy nourished a remarkable confluence of inventors, entrepreneurs, visionary venture capitalists - and an entire society eager to embrace the promise of the new mechanical brains. The results were staggering: the IBM 360; the integrated circuit; and the microprocessor are just three of the world-altering results. **We pay tribute here not only to the inventors of these marvelous devices, but to the pioneering entrepreneurs and communicators who helped drive the industry and shape its destiny.**

Wizards and Their Wonders is not meant to be definitive. It does, however, represent a core group of American inventors and entrepreneurs whose contributions to the computing field are indisputable. As with any such compendium, many worthy names had to be left out. Owing to time constraints and scheduling conflicts, we were unable to photograph Paul Allen, Dave Cutler, and Bill Joy, among others. We regret the omissions. Our goal is also not to minimize the considerable – and often seminal – contributions made by scores of non-American computing innovators. Charles Babbage and Alan Turing come immediately to mind. Significantly, the most prized award in computing, which has been won by many of our inductees, is the ACM's Turing Award. We hope in the future to create a companion tribute to these computer innovators such as Niklaus Wirth, Maurice Wilkes, Konrad Zuse, and so on.

Because the computing business gets a lot of press, **a few of the people represented here will be familiar to almost everyone. Others may surprise even insiders.** Names like Bill Gates – known to all the world – are juxtaposed with other important names known primarily to insiders and aficionados. This is in part because the selection process was from the inside out. The Computer Museum began assembling the "Wizards" list by first identifying those who had won the National Medal of Technology and/or other prestigious awards in the computing field. That group in turn helped to nominate others in the field who have made significant contribution. And so the list grew, spreading beyond the core group of inventors to include entrepreneurs, communicators, and venture capitalists and bankers.

What stands out more than anything else in this compendium is the team approach to innovation. The computer business is constantly creating and updating software and hardware. This requires multi-talented teams of people from many disciplines working in synergy to keep the gears turning at a speedy pace. Such interdisciplinary teamwork is perhaps unprecedented in the history of technology. **The inventors spur on the entrepreneurs, who in turn feed their energies back to the inventors. The communicators oil the wheels through encouragement and criticism.** The mad pace creates a multi-player "organism," if you will.

Wizards and Their Wonders also pays tribute to a key group of "Forerunners" – such as John von Neumann and Grace Murray Hopper, without whom the computer would be very different today. It's hard to imagine where we would be without von Neumann's concept of the stored program or Hopper's pioneering work in compiler design.

An initial exhibition of the "Inventors" portraits, also called "Wizards and Their Wonders," was held in March, 1997, at the San Jose Convention Center in San Jose, California, in conjunction with the ACM97 conference and Exposition on "The Next Fifty Years of Computing," a celebration of the 50th anniversary of the ACM (Association for Computing Machinery). The exhibit was sponsored by The Computer Museum's History Center. Tens of thousands of people attended the exhibition and viewed the Bachrach portraits, as well as the many accompanying artifacts generously loaned from private collections. Among them were: a framed Apple 1 board on loan from Scott Cook; one of the first core memory planes from Jay Forrester's Whirlwind computer; and a console from an IBM 360/40 mainframe computer. Also featured was the prototype of the Busicom calculator, the first commercial product containing a microprocessor, the Intel 4004. Photographs of these artifacts appear herein. The exhibit gave people a chance to look back on the past fifty years as they begin to speculate about the next fifty. We hope this book will do the same.

ACKNOWLEDGMENTS

This book was assembled in just a few "Internet years," and could not have happened without a remarkable team effort. I am grateful to all of you. Thanks to: Gwen Bell, for the initial impetus to create "Wizards," and her unflagging help throughout the process; to Joseph DeBlasi, Mark Mandelbaum, and Lynn D'Addesio at the ACM, for their continued support; to Louis Fabian Bachrach, for his remarkable photographs; to James Burke, for kindly agreeing to write the Introduction; to Gill Fishman and Christopher Frame of Gill Fishman Associates for the elegant book design and their patient forbearance; to Dag Spicer of The Computer Museum History Center, who, with Gwen Bell, wrote most of the initial drafts for the biographical sketches in the "Inventors" chapter, and who helped hunt down artifact photographs; to Francine McNeill, for excellent copy editing done under tight deadlines; and to Oliver Strimpel, Carol Welsh, Zoe Allison, and Gail Jennes of The Computer Museum. Thanks also goes to the "Wizards" themselves and their support staffs for making biographical information available to us so promptly. I would also like to thank David Seuss of Northern Light, who gave me early access to the beta version of the Northern Light search engine (www.nlsearch.com). It proved invaluable in tracking down elusive information.

Thanks, finally, to those who run the Internet or who provide the information contained on it. Without them, this book would have been impossible to research and compile so quickly.

– C.M.

Introduction

by James Burke

Sometime around seventeen thousand years ago, in a cave in Southern France, the magic wand first appeared. It foretold the future. And it endowed with supernatural power the shaman-wizard who used it. The wand, now known to archeologists as the Montgaudier Baton, was made of antler horn and carved with tiny markings indicating the phases of the Moon from the time of thaw, when the group could leave the protection of the cave to hunt and gather, to the time of freeze, when they would need to re-enter the cave in order to survive the winter. The Baton also bore carved outlines of animals and plants. It was, in effect, a calendar, and the shaman-wizard who was able to read the signs carved on it wielded supreme authority because his magic wand told him where and when the tribe should go out and find food.

Twelve thousand years later the same kind of power lay in the hands of men who would, on one occasion, make mysterious marks in wet clay tablets and then, years later, needed only to look at those marks in order magically to remember everything that had happened when the marks were originally made. These "lookers" founded the first cities and wrote the first laws to govern the inhabitants, who could not read cuneiform pictographs.

Three thousand five hundred years ago, at a turquoise mine in the Sinai Peninsula, a Phoenician worker scratched simple sound symbols on a rock and split society between the tiny minority who knew the alphabet and the vast majority who did not.

In 1450, Johann Gutenberg made alphabetic letters of metal and completed the process begun in the caves. Thanks to books, esoteric information could now be more easily shared, in portable, printed form, among the very few widely-separated individuals who possessed it. In time, the necessary collation and verification of printed information by the new editing houses would bring into existence the most powerful tool in history for generating even more data. Within two hundred years of the printing press, Rene Descartes would invent a foolproof, reductionist technique for analyzing data. Its effect would be to cause the body of knowledge to proliferate into a myriad of disciplines, each with their shaman-wizards, each using incomprehensible notation and vocabulary that only initiates could read. And each, thanks to print, is now growing at an accelerating rate.

The modern world is the product of this millennial process, from cave to science, of the exclusion of the majority. **The miracles of science and technology with which we live today have emerged from a mode of thought that has increasingly required the specialist to know more and more about less and less.** The inevitable corollary has been that the vast majority of non-specialists has found itself knowing less and less about more and more.

That this profoundly undemocratic system should, through technology, have provided humankind with a democracy of possessions is almost entirely due to the pulling power of the marketplace and the driving force of consumer demand. In consequence, since the eighteenth-century Industrial Revolution, the frustration that might have arisen from political and social disfranchisement through ignorance, has been largely offset by the continued fulfillment of rising material expectations.

However, thirty years ago, that sense of frustration began to find expression, as the effects of information technology became more widespread. Television appeared to show people that the old institutions were no longer adequate; that the old certainties were questionable; that life was too complex for simple choices, either at the ballot box or in the examination room; that the time had come for a fundamental change in the way in which knowledge was generated and in what way it was socially implemented.

It is one of the fascinations of the historical process that, even while science and technology were creating this problem for the early twenty-first century, they were also providing the means for its solution. Over the last hundred years a number of discoveries have been made which, at the time, would have appeared entirely unrelated to each other, and to this present-day issue. Those developments and inventions included such things as artillery tables, fiberglass, the use of a perforated card for loom control, the DEWLINE radar defense network, crystal manufacture, lasers, spaceflight, nuclear explosion mathematical models, and others too numerous to mention.

Today, these advances have coalesced into a new technology of computing that will radically change the pattern of history as it has unfolded so far. For the first time, affordable universal access to information will be possible. Nobody knows what the effect will be. Since the time of the first flint tool there has never been an informed, enfranchised majority. **The power and responsibility that comes with knowledge has never been placed in so many hands.** The means of self-expression has never been so readily available to so many different cultures around the world.

Informationally, we are – as it were – about to come out of the cave once again. But this time the shaman-wizards will point the way, rather than lead; they will serve, rather than command; empower, rather than enslave. And this time they will not be remote, mysterious figures with awesome, magical powers to deny and exclude. They will be the men and women whose vision and talent have prepared for this moment of change. They are the people who, collectively, have brought about the invention of the computer or who foster its development. People who will make it possible for the meaning of: "communication" to return to its original sense: "to share." These are the people whose work will shape the twenty-first century. People like the wizards you will find in this book.

Forerunners

2

Like the camera and the television set, the computer has no sole "inventor." It is the result of a series of technological breakthroughs on the part of Napier, Leibniz, Pascal, Babbage, Boole, and many others, culminating in work done by the people in this chapter – a classic example of James Burke's idea of technological "connections:" a series of technical advances leading to a sometimes unexpected conclusion. We celebrate the twentieth century American pioneers who built the foundation for the modern computer, and acknowledge the many important advances in computing that occurred in other countries as well – Alan Turing's work in England being just one example. Kennedy's quote above came at a time when the United States mainframe computer industry was in its prime, dominating the world market. The industry was at the beginning of a success curve that would see many new records broken in the coming decades, spurred on by a quintessentially American phenomenon: the microprocessor. Here are the one-of-a-kind, tenacious pioneers who helped make it happen.

Howard
AIKEN

Howard Aiken (1900-1973) was responsible for the pioneering Mark I computer at Harvard University, the first of America's "giant brains," as Edmund Berkeley described the behemoths in 1949. The Mark I was officially known as the IBM Automatic Sequence-Controlled Calculator. It began operating in April 1944 and used relays rather than vacuum tubes. Grace Murray Hopper said, "Aiken was never really given the credit for the first large-scale digital computer, even if it was built out of step counters and relays."

"Don't worry about people stealing an idea. If it's original, you'll have to jam it down their throats."

John ATANASOFF

John Atanasoff (1903-1995) has been called the true unsung
"father" of the computer, having won the legal right to the title
after bringing suit against J. Presper Eckert and John Mauchly
(of ENIAC fame) in the early 1970s. In the eyes of many
historians, the controversy may never be completely settled,
but Atanasoff clearly played a vital role in the evolution of the
digital computer. He had an epiphany in 1937 in a tavern
during a high-speed car trip across Iowa where, after two
bourbons, he decided to create an electronic computer based
on the binary number system. It would use capacitors as
memory devices and would compute by direct logical action
instead of by enumeration. In 1939, Atanasoff and Clifford
Berry built a prototype, which worked in a limited fashion. It
no longer exists. Atanasoff received a Ph.D. degree in physics
from the University of Wisconsin and won many awards,
including the National Medal of Technology.

"Every damn thing worked. We didn't have much to deal with, but everything worked. . .
With me the accomplishment is getting the ideas. As soon as you got the ideas,
anybody could build it." – JOHN ATANASOFF, DESCRIBING HIS 1939 PROTOTYPE

Seymour
CRAY

In 1964, Seymour Cray (1925-1996) developed the Control Data CDC 6600, arguably the first supercomputer. He went on to design the CRAY-1 supercomputer in the 1970s, a pioneering device that could process data at 80 megaflops (millions of floating-point instructions per second), an unheard-of rate at the time. It was horseshoe-shaped to minimize the physical limitation of the speed of light, which governed the passage of current in its wiring. He later designed many successors to the CRAY-1, and won both the IEEE Computer Society Pioneer Award and the ACM/IEEE Eckert-Mauchly Award. The reclusive Cray was also eccentric. According to Robert Slater, when Cray needed a new car, he would "pick the first car to the right on the showroom floor."

The Cray -1 Supercomputer

J. Presper
ECKERT

In the early 1940s, with John Mauchly, J. Presper Eckert (1919-1995) co-invented the ENIAC, the first successful electronic digital computer, and was the Chief Engineer on the project. The ENIAC sported 17,468 vacuum tubes and could perform about 36 multiplications per second. In addition to the ENIAC, Eckert and Mauchly developed the UNIVAC, BINAC, and EDVAC computers. Eckert received an M.S. degree from the Moore School of the University of Pennsylvania, and won the IEEE Computer Society Pioneer Award, among others. Later in his life, he pursued his avid interest in high-fidelity sound reproduction.

Grace Murray
HOPPER

Grace Murray Hopper (1906-1992) is, in Charlene Billings's phrase, "the grandmother of the computer age." Her friends called her "Amazing Grace." She was a seminal influence on modern computing, developing software for the Mark I and the UNIVAC I computers, and leading the development of compilers for the COBOL language. She served as a Rear Admiral in the U.S. Navy. Fond of whimsy, she cataloged the first computer "bug" – a moth that flew into a Mark I relay and caused the machine to malfunction. The list of her awards and degrees exceeds two full pages, including the National Medal of Technology and thirty-seven honorary doctoral degrees. She received a Ph.D. degree from Yale University in 1930.

"The American people finally adopted the term [programmer] because, I think,
it sounded elegant and they thought that 'programmers' would make
more money than 'coders.'"

John
KEMENY

During the 1960s, with Thomas Kurtz, John Kemeny (1926-1992) co-developed the most popular computer language in history – BASIC. The "Beginner's All-Purpose Symbolic Instruction Code" was part of a revolutionary plan by the two Dartmouth College mathematics professors to make computers accessible to students on campus via time-share terminals. BASIC was more accessible and understandable than the programming alternatives then available, and it became popular with students from all disciplines. It later propelled the development of personal computing software. Kemeny began his career as a graduate student assistant to Albert Einstein, checking the physicist's calculations.

John MAUCHLY

With J. Presper Eckert in the 1940s, John Mauchly (1907-1980) co-invented the ENIAC, the first successful electronic digital computer. The U.S. Army funded the ENIAC's development to calculate ballistics tables, among other top secret tasks. Another co-invention of Mauchly and Eckert, the UNIVAC I, was the first computer to successfully predict the outcome of a U.S. election (Eisenhower's) in 1952. Many historians claim that John Atanasoff was the true "inventor" of the digital computer; others credit Mauchly and Eckert with having the necessary drive and initiative to get the job done. Mauchly received a Ph.D. degree in physics from Johns Hopkins University, and won many awards, including the IEEE Computer Society Pioneer Award.

Allen
NEWELL

Allen Newell (1927-1992) was a pioneer in artificial intelligence and developed the "rule-based' approach to problem solving. J. A. N. Lee notes that Newell believed "computers could process symbols as well as numbers and, if programmed properly, would be capable of solving problems in the same way humans do." He taught at Carnegie-Mellon and played a key role in developing the computer science department there. Among his many awards is the ACM's Turing Award and the Franklin Institute's Louis E. Levy medal. With Gordon Bell, Newell wrote *Computer Structures*, a classic computer science text. He received a Ph.D. degree in industrial administration from the Carnegie Institute of Technology.

George
STIBITZ

George Stibitz (1904-1995) worked at Bell Telephone Laboratories in the 1930s, where he created several pioneering relay-based computers. His machines grew out of an initial experiment in building a one-digit binary adder from a tobacco can, plywood, two dry cell batteries, and bulbs. The gadget was a source of amusement to his colleagues, but from it Stibitz created the larger framework for a computing device that could do real work. Of almost equal importance, his relay machines could be operated remotely over telephone lines using a Teletype machine. Stibitz then began work on a desktop computer project, which was never completed. He later became involved in teaching.

John von NEUMANN

John von Neumann (1903-1957) developed the stored program concept of computing and, with Alan Turing, is one of the two towering influences in the development of computers in this century. He created the logical design for the early IAS (Institute for Advanced Studies) computer at Princeton University, using the now-famous "von Neumann architecture." Historian Nancy Stern notes that von Neumann's brilliant contributions were both technical and sociological, helping in the latter case to legitimize the use of computers for scientific and engineering work. His "First Draft of a Report on the EDVAC" is one of the classic papers in computing, and his collected works on mathematics fill six volumes. He received a Ph.D. degree in mathematics from the University of Budapest and many honors, including the Enrico Fermi Award and the Medal of Freedom. He died in 1957, leaving unfinished a brief series of lectures about computers that he had hoped to deliver at Yale University.

Thomas J.
WATSON, JR.

Almost from birth, Thomas J. Watson, Jr. (1914-1993) was fated to take over the International Business Machines Corporation (IBM) from his pioneering father, Thomas J. Watson, Sr. During Watson Jr.'s tenure as President and Chairman from 1952 until 1979, IBM grew to dominate the worldwide computing market completely. He stressed leasing rather than selling mainframe computers, and raised the arts of salesmanship and service to new heights. He oversaw the birth of the System/360 computer, which, with its successor machines, remains the most financially successful line of computers in history. He received a B.A. degree from Brown University. After retiring from IBM, he served as U.S. Ambassador to the Soviet Union from 1979 to 1988.

Thomas J.
WATSON, SR.

Thomas J. Watson, Sr. (1874-1956), founded the International Business Machines Corporation (IBM) in the 1920s, which grew out of the Computing-Tabulating-Recording Corporation. He began his career selling pianos and sewing machines, and helped launch the era of computers in business by acting as prime contractor for Howard Aiken's MARK I project at Harvard University. Watson originated the famous IBM motto, "Think," and was a supreme business strategist. He turned over the reins to his son somewhat reluctantly in 1952. He is said to have predicted a world market of "maybe five computers" in the 1940s, but recent research indicates the quote is almost certainly apocryphal. He never received a college degree.

Inventors

"The best way to predict the future is to invent it." – ALAN KAY

One of the benefits of the fast rate of computer development is that many of the industry's primary inventors are still very much alive and active, and could be photographed and interviewed for this celebration. It is perhaps the first technology in which we have the luxury of actually meeting the people who created its key inventions, in this case, the mouse, the laser printer, the Internet, the World Wide Web, the word processor, the Ethernet, the spreadsheet, and the graphical user interface. Though some of the people in this chapter will be well-known to many readers, you may be pleasantly surprised to connect a face with a name for the first time. In this chapter you will meet the people who helped create the wonders we use every day - the inventors of the modern computer.

inventors

Fran
ALLEN

Fran Allen is an IBM Fellow at IBM's Thomas J. Watson
Research Laboratory. She specializes in compilers, compiler
optimization, and high-performance systems. Her early work
led to algorithms and technologies that are the basis for the
theory of program optimization. In 1978, John Backus said
that the work done by Allen and John Cocke in developing
early FORTRAN compilers was "incredible. It is very unusual
for any technical achievement to remain the best in its field for
even five years, and yet the FORTRAN I compiler has
remained the best overall optimizer for 20 years." She was
inducted into the Women in Technology International
(WITI) Hall of Fame in 1997 for her early programming
work. She is a member of the National Academy of
Engineering and a Fellow of both the Association for
Computing Machinery (ACM) and the IEEE.

**Fran Allen's 1964 paper on "Program
Optimization," prepared for IBM's
Thomas J. Watson Research Center.**

PROGRAM OPTIMIZATION

F. E. Allen

IBM Watson Research Center
Yorktown Heights, New York

ABSTRACT: Machine independent and language independent methods
of optimizing the execution times of compiled programs are described.
The approach is based on the topological characteristics of a program.
A program partitioning into "strongly connected" regions is developed
which permits modular optimization. The principal methods considered
are eliminating redundant instructions, folding, moving instructions
from one part of the program to another, reducing the strength of
operators, replacing tests, and eliminating unused definitions and the
computations upon which they depend. These techniques are described
in enough detail to permit an evaluation of their compile time costs
and the improvements they make in the object code. The appendices
contain examples of programs run on the compiler which embodies the
methods.

"We are still designing compilers using techniques **developed in [the first FORTRAN]**
project. The code sets a standard for object-code efficiency
and for feasibility of using high-level languages."

– FRAN ALLEN, ON THE 25TH ANNIVERSARY OF FORTRAN, 1982

Marc ANDREESSEN

Marc Andreessen is Senior Vice President of Technology for Netscape Communications. Andreessen developed the idea for the NCSA Mosaic browser for the Internet in the fall of 1992 while he was an undergraduate student at the University of Illinois and a staff member at the university's National Center for Supercomputing Applications in Champaign, Illinois. In his role at Netscape Communications, he oversees the technical direction of the company. He received a B.S. degree in computer science from the University of Illinois in 1993, and was named one of the top 50 people under age 40 by *Time* magazine in 1994.

Jim Barksdale is President and CEO of Netscape. Prior to that he was Chief Executive Officer of AT&T Wireless Services, working in wireless communications. He was also President and Chief Operating Officer of McCaw, and spent twelve years with Federal Express Corporation of Memphis, Tennessee, as Chief Information Officer, overseeing the development and implementation of the company's pioneering customer service and package tracking systems. In 1983, he became Executive Vice President and COO. Under his leadership, Federal Express became the first service company to receive the Malcolm Baldridge National Quality Award.

James BARKSDALE

33

"Marc Andreessen had barely come of age when he co-wrote the program
that is **helping to tame the Internet** . . . he is often cited as one of the
few people who have a road map for the 'infobahn.'"– TIME MAGAZINE

Charles W. BACHMAN

Charles (Charlie) W. Bachman has been called the "father of database management" and is the inventor of data structure diagrams and data modeling. Bachman developed the Integrated Data Store, the first successful database management system and the basis for several commercial products, including Honeywell's IDS II, Cullinet's IDMS, and Sperry's DMS 1100 database management systems. He also invented the CODASYL database systems now running on every type of large computer in the world. He is also widely known for the Bachman diagrams used frequently in database design activities.

He is a founder of Cayenne Software, Inc., a Bachman Cadre company, an ACM Turing Award Laureate (1973), and a Distinguished Fellow of the British Computer Society (1978). He holds many U.S. and foreign patents.

John
BACKUS

John Backus led a team at IBM in 1957 that created the first
successful high-level programming language, FORTRAN. It
was designed to solve problems in science and engineering,
and many dialects of the language are still in use throughout
the world. Describing the development of FORTRAN,
Backus said "We simply made up the language as we went
along. We did not regard language design as a difficult problem, merely a simple prelude to the real problem: designing a
compiler which could produce efficient programs . . . . We also
wanted to eliminate a lot of the bookkeeping and detailed,
repetitive planning which hand coding involved." The name
FORTRAN comes from FORmula TRANslation. The language was designed for solving engineering and scientific
problems. FORTRAN IV was first introduced by IBM in the
early 1960s and still exists in a number of similar dialects on
machines from various manufacturers.

Daniel McCracken's

early book on FORTRAN.

DANIEL D. McCRACKEN
a guide to
FORTRAN
programming

"[In the 1950s] programming and debugging **accounted for**
as much as three quarters of the cost of operating a computer.
This economic factor was one of the prime motivations which led me to propose
the FORTRAN project."

Paul
BARAN

Paul Baran was born in 1926 and began his professional career as a technician working on the UNIVAC I computer at the Eckert-Mauchly Computer Company in 1949. In the 1960s, he founded the Institute for the Future, a non-profit research organization dedicated to developing longer-range planning methodologies. In the 1970s, he formed Cabledata Associates, which in turn launched Comprint, Equatorial Communications Company (the first VSAT company), and Telebit, which was based on a technology invented by Baran called orthogonal discrete multitone modulation (ODMT) and which created the fastest modem of its time.

Baran is currently the Chairman of the Board of Com21. He is the recipient of numerous awards, including the Computers and Communications Award (with Vint Cerf and Tim Berners-Lee), the ACM Special Interest Group in Communications First Annual Award, and the Electronic Frontier Foundation Pioneer Award. He is a Life Fellow of the IEEE.

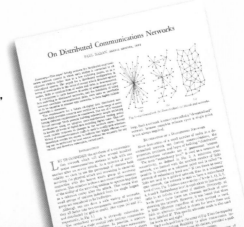

Paul Baran's pioneering paper, "On Distributed Communications Networks."

Forrest
BASKETT

Forrest Baskett is currently Senior Vice-President of Research and Development and Chief Technology Officer at Silicon Graphics, Inc. (SGI), Mountain View, California. Baskett served as a Professor of Computer Science and Electrical Engineering for eleven years at Stanford University, and spent two years leading a team that developed an operating system for the Cray 1 supercomputer at Los Alamos National Laboratory. He was also a member of the MIPS processor design team at Stanford and a Principal Scientist at the Xerox Palo Alto Research Center (PARC) investigating parallel and reduced instruction set computer (RISC) processors. He holds a B.A. degree in mathematics from Rice University and a Ph.D. degree in computer science from the University of Texas at Austin.

"The real challenge facing computer designers over the next 10 years will be

how to take advantage of all that computing power.

Device designs are now getting so complex that we're becoming seriously limited by the

ability to effectively manage that complexity."

Andreas
BECHTOLSHEIM

While a graduate student at Stanford University in 1981, Andreas Bechtolsheim designed a workstation for himself using off-the-shelf parts. Using $25,000 of his own money to build prototypes, he soon attracted the attention of Vinod Khosla and Scott McNealy, two Stanford University M.B.A. students. The trio then recruited Bill Joy, principal architect of the Berkeley Standard Distribution (BSD) Unix operating system, and founded Sun Microsystems. The name Sun originally stood for "Stanford University Network."

Gordon
BELL

Gordon Bell spent twenty-three years at Digital Equipment Corporation as Vice President of Engineering. At Digital, he was responsible for the first mini- and time-sharing computer, and led the development of the VAX. The first Assistant Director for Computing at NSF, Bell headed the National Research Network panel that became the National Information Infrastructure (NII). He is the author of the *High Performance Computer and Communications Initiative*, and co-authored *Computer Structures: Readings and Examples* with Allen Newell. Bell is the recipient of the 1991 National Medal of Technology. Currently, he is Senior Researcher at Microsoft Research Corp.

The PDP-6, shown with Gordon Bell (left) and Alan Kotok. The 36-bit PDP-6 was delivered in 1964 to MIT's Project MAC, the University of Western Australia, Brookhaven National Laboratory, and Lawrence Livermore National Laboratory. It was the first of the personal "mainframes" designed for both time-sharing and real-time laboratory applications. Kotok went on to develop the follow-on PDP-10.

"For short-term predictions, **bet against the optimist.**"

Tim BERNERS-LEE

Tim Berners-Lee, World Wide Web developer, trained in physics at Oxford. In 1990, he was working at the Swiss-based European Particle Physics Laboratory (CERN) when he wrote the specifications for the global hypermedia system, using the then innocuous acronyms HTTP, HTML, and URL. In 1994, Berners-Lee left CERN to found the World Wide Web Consortium, a non-profit group of research institutions, Web technology users, and providers based at MIT's Laboratory for Computer Science. In commenting on the World Wide Web, Berners-Lee has said "The Internet, specifically the Web, is moving from appearing as a neat application to being the underlying information space in which we communicate, learn, compute, and do business."

Tim Berners-Lee's original paper that led to the World Wide Web: "Information Management: A Proposal" for a distributed hypertext system.

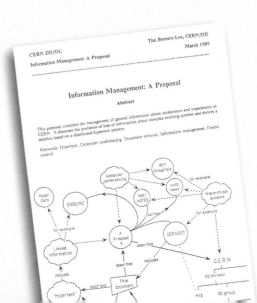

"'Web' [stands for the Web's] decentralized nonhierarchical topology,

which is key, and **'World Wide' goes better with 'Web' than does 'global'** . . .

I got a lot of grief for making an acronym with more syllables than the name itself."

— TIM BERNERS-LEE, ON NAMING THE WORLD WIDE WEB

Joel
BIRNBAUM

Dr. Joel Birnbaum graduated with a Bachelor's degree in engineering physics from Cornell University in 1960 and M.S. and Ph.D. degrees in nuclear physics from Yale University in 1965. He began working at IBM's Thomas J. Watson Research Laboratory where he last served as Director of Computer Sciences. His research interests lie in the areas of real-time data acquisition and RISC processor architecture. He joined Hewlett-Packard in 1980 as founding Director of the HP Laboratories Research Center. In 1988, he was appointed Vice-President and General Manager of HP's Information Architecture Group, which developed the PA-RISC architecture.

"[A future quantum computer] could offer extraordinary parallelism.
With just 800 calculating "gates" – dramatically fewer than commonly found on
leading-edge chips today – **it could do simultaneous calculations on
more numbers than there are protons in the known universe.**"

Jim
BLINN

Jim Blinn has been involved in computer graphics since 1967 and has devoted most of his career to using computer graphics in various educational projects. He is a Graphics Fellow (with Alvy Ray Smith) of the Computer Graphics Research group at Microsoft Research Corp. He is the recipient of many awards, including the first SIGGRAPH Computer Graphics Achievement Award for work in lighting and surface modeling techniques, and the NASA Exceptional Service medal for his remarkable Voyager fly-by animations. He writes *Jim Blinn's Corner*, a lighthearted regular column in *IEEE Computer Graphics and Applications*. At Caltech he also produced *Project Mathematics!*, a series of animated videotapes to teach high school mathematics. Being partial to Dr. Seuss, Blinn takes a whimsical approach to science that, according to *Wired* magazine, "rests on a serious bedrock of obsession."

"For the first 16 years of my career I spent my time developing the tools of computer graphics. But then I realized that **few people remember who invented oil paints; most people remember the artists who use them**. So for the past 12 years I have been using tools rather than building them."

Erich BLOCH

In 1952, Erich Bloch joined IBM and worked on making ferrite core memory manufacturable and creating the first commercially successful million-bit memory. He headed IBM's Solid Logic Technology (SLT) program used in the System/360 computer and shared the National Medal of Technology in 1985 with co-developers Bob Evans and Fred Brooks, Jr. The System/360 remains the most popular family of computers ever built. In 1948, Bloch emigrated to the United States from Switzerland. He took night courses while working at menial jobs during the day, and earned a B.E.E. degree from the University of Buffalo.

The Solid Logic Technology (SLT) module, the basic electronic building block of the IBM System/360 Computer.

Leonard
BOSACK

Leonard Bosack co-founded Cisco Systems in 1984 with Sandy Lerner. At the time, Bosack was Director of Computer Facilities for Stanford's Department of Computer Science, and Lerner was Director of Computer Facilities for Stanford's Graduate School of Business. Cisco was formed to commercialize Stanford University's SUNet (Stanford University Network), developed in the late 1970s as their campus-wide network, and to combine several local networks into one large network. Bosack is currently the President and Owner of XKL LLC in Redmond, Washington. He received an M.S. degree in computer science from Stanford University.

Dan
BRICKLIN

Dan Bricklin, an electrical engineering graduate from MIT in
1973, began working for Digital Equipment Corporation as a
programmer. He later left Digital to enter Harvard Business
School. In the late 1970s, he teamed up with old MIT friend
Bob Frankston to create the world's first electronic spreadsheet,
VisiCalc. The software was inspired by Bricklin's personal
experience at Harvard with "running the numbers" to
determine company financial health by performing many
laborious computations. *VisiCalc* first appeared for the
Apple II computer, greatly accelerating that computer's sales.
By 1983, over 500,000 copies of *VisiCalc* had been sold.

Some examples of *VisiCalc* packaging

"[With VisiCalc], we were making the **users do**

more of the programming, but they didn't know it."

Fred
BROOKS, JR.

Fred Brooks, Jr., was 29 when he joined IBM and was put in charge of System/360. He shared the National Medal of Technology in 1985 with Erich Bloch and Bob Evans. He is the author of *The Mythical Man-Month* (1975), an important book about software engineering incorporating Brooks' Law, which states that, "Adding manpower to a late software project makes it later." According to Bob Metcalfe, "Mr. Brooks saw his law operating at IBM in the 1960s, when the joke was that if IBM asked its programmers to jump a 100-foot gorge, a hundred of them would each jump one foot." In 1956, he graduated from Harvard University with a Ph.D. degree in mathematic, studying with Howard Aiken and working on the Harvard Mark I computer.

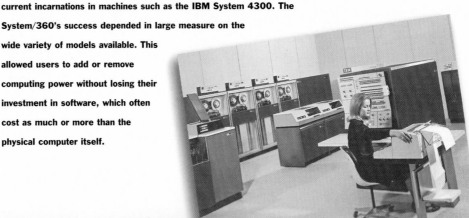

The IBM System/360 Model 40. The System/360 series generated over $100 billion in revenue for IBM from its product launch in April 1964, to its current incarnations in machines such as the IBM System 4300. The System/360's success depended in large measure on the wide variety of models available. This allowed users to add or remove computing power without losing their investment in software, which often cost as much or more than the physical computer itself.

"**The tar pit of software engineering** will continue to be sticky for a long time to come."

Bruce G.
BUCHANAN

Bruce G. Buchanan is Professor of Computer Science, Philosophy, and Medicine with the Department of Computer Science at the University of Pittsburgh. He is also Co-Director of the Keck Center for Advanced Training in Computational Biology. His main research interests are in machine learning, knowledge-based systems, medical expert systems, and computational biology. He is also interested in applications of machine learning and artificial intelligence to any problems in biology or medicine. His most recent research is in artificial intelligence approaches to machine learning and applications of symbolic learning to problems in biology and medicine.

Ed CATMULL

At Lucasfilm, Ed Catmull created special effects for the movie *Star Trek II: The Wrath of Khan*. He was a key developer of Renderman software, used in such Hollywood films as *The Abyss, Terminator II, Jurassic Park, Jumanji, Beauty and the Beast, Batman II,* and *Toy Story*. In 1996, he received an Academy Award from the Academy of Motion Picture Arts and Sciences for scientific and technical engineering contributions to the evolution of computer graphics in filmmaking. He graduated from the University of Utah with a Ph.D. degree in computer science, specializing in computer graphics.

Vint
CERF

Vint Cerf, known as the "father of the Internet," is the co-developer of the computer networking protocol TCP/IP, now the transmission standard for data communications on the Internet. Much of Cerf's early work was undertaken during the period from 1976 to 1982, when he worked on the DARPA project for the Department of Defense. He holds a B.S. degree in mathematics from Stanford University and M.S. and Ph.D. degrees from UCLA. Cerf is now Senior Vice-President of Internet Architecture and Engineering at MCI Corporation.

The ARPA network in December, 1969, showing the four existing nodes at SRI, UCSB, UCLA, and Utah.

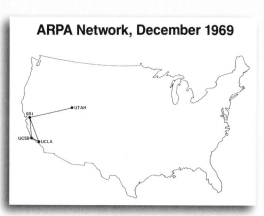

ARPA Network, December 1969

"We're a society that wants everything, **and we want it now**. I think that's what the Internet is responding to."

John CHOWNING

John Chowning is best known for having discovered the frequency modulation (FM) algorithm, a breakthrough in the synthesis of musical timbres that, according to Robert Willey, "allowed for a very simple, yet elegant way of creating and controlling time-varying spectra." In 1973, he and Stanford University began a relationship with Yamaha in Japan, which led to the most successful synthesizer series in the history of electronic musical instruments. Chowning studied with Leland Smith at Stanford University in the 1960s, where he received a doctorate in composition, and today continues to compose music.

"[At Yamaha we created] a generalized keyboard that can be particularized to any desired piano or any specific piano. **If you want a fortepiano of, say, the 1780s, you can have it,** and the sound that goes with it."

inventors

Wes CLARK

In 1951, Wes Clark joined the MIT Digital Computer Laboratory as a Whirlwind computer programmer. Over the next twelve years, he was principal architect of the TX-0, TX-2, L-1, ARC-1, and LINC computers. From 1964 to 1972, Clark led Washington University's ARPA/NIH project on macromodular systems with Dr. Charles Molnar. Subsequently, he formed the New York consulting firm of Clark, Rockoff and Associates.

The LINC Computer

John
COCKE

At IBM, John Cocke developed the concept of reduced instruction set computer (RISC) technology, a cornerstone of high-speed computer design, relying on a minimal instruction set and highly efficient compiler design. He was a multifaceted talent at IBM, working on compilers, and inventing the concept of "look-ahead" for the IBM Stretch computer. He has inspired generations of engineers. He has won both the National Medal of Technology (1991) and the National Medal of Science (1994), as well as the ACM Turing Award (1985) for this innovation. He graduated in 1956 from Duke University with a Ph.D. degree in mathematics.

Fernando CORBATÓ

In 1963, Fernando Corbató became group leader at the Laboratory for Computer Science at MIT, where he and his colleagues wrote the first compatible time-sharing operating system, which evolved into Multics, allowing many users to interact with the large mainframe computers of the day. He received his Ph.D. degree in physics from MIT in 1956. He has received many honors, including the ACM Turing Award. He also won the W. W. McDowell and the Harry Goode Memorial Awards, both for his work in developing time-sharing systems.

Whitfield
DIFFIE

Whitfield Diffie developed the concept of public key cryptography in 1975. Prior to becoming interested in cryptography, he worked on the development of the MathLab symbolic manipulation system and, later on, proof of correctness of computer programs at Stanford University. From 1979 until 1991, Diffie was Manager of Secure Systems Research at Northern Telecom. In 1991, he began working at Sun Microsystems, where he is a Distinguished Engineer. Diffie also consults on "crypto-politics," having testified twice to the Senate and twice to the House on computer security policy. He was awarded the inaugural ACM Paris Kanellakis Theory and Practice Award in 1997. He received a B.S. degree in mathematics from MIT in 1965.

Douglas
ENGELBART

Douglas Engelbart is best known for his pioneering work during the 1960s and 1970s developing computing technologies that have since become commonplace – the mouse, hypertext, windows, cross-file editing, and mixed text and graphics files. In partnership with Sun Microsystems and Netscape Communications, he is pursuing his long-standing interest in boosting human intelligence, first laid out in his 1962 paper, "Augmenting Human Intellect: A Conceptual Framework." Engelbart graduated with a Ph.D. degree in electrical engineering from the University of California, Berkeley, in 1957, and is the holder of approximately two dozen patents. In describing Engelbart's contributions, EECS Department Chair Randy Katz (University of California, Berkeley) says that Engelbart's ideas "are aimed not so much at creating new technology, but at making people's lives better – the ultimate accolade for an engineer."

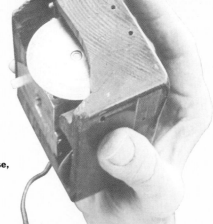

Doug Engelbart's first mouse, built in 1964.

Joseph F. ENGELBERGER

Joseph F. Engelberger, often called the "father of robotics," and George Devol co-founded the world's first robot company, Unimation, in 1954. Devol predicted that the industrial robot would "help the factory operator in a way that can be compared to business machines as an aid to the office worker." A few years later, in 1961, the very first industrial robot was "employed" in a General Motors automobile factory in New Jersey. Since 1980, there has been an expansion of industrial robots into non-automotive industries. One factor responsible for this growth has been the technical improvements in robots due to advancement in microelectronics and computers. Engelberger has won many awards, including the Leonardo da Vinci award of the American Society of Mechanical Engineers.

Joseph F. Engelberger speaks to students at the Computer Museum in 1993 about their robotic creations for a project. Engelberger's Unimate robot is shown at left, rear.

Edward A.
FEIGENBAUM

Edward A. Feigenbaum, one of the early innovators in artificial intelligence, has been a major force in software innovation since the 1960s, when he and his team developed the first expert system, DENDRAL. Subsequently, he and his group developed a wide variety of applications, learning programs, and software development systems for expert systems. He graduated with a Ph.D. degree in industrial administration from Carnegie-Mellon University's Institute of Technology in 1960, and won the 1995 ACM Turing Award in conjunction with Raj Reddy for his work on large-scale artificial-intelligence systems. He has served as Chief Scientist of the Air Force, advising the Secretary and Chief of Staff on matters related to science and the technologies.

Edward A. Feigenbaum's pioneering collection of papers on Artificial Intelligence from the early 1970's, *Computers and Thought*, co-edited by Feigenbaum, Julian Feldman, and Paul Armer.

COMPUTERS
AND THOUGHT

Armer	Hansen	Selfridge
Chomsky	Hovland	Shaw
Clarkson	Hunt	Simon
Feigenbaum	Laughery	Slagle
Feldman	Lindsay	Tonge
Gelernter	Loveland	Turing
Green	Minsky	Uhr
Gullahorn	Neisser	Vossler
Gullahorn	Newell	Wolf
	Samuel	

Edited by EDWARD A. FEIGENBAUM
and JULIAN FELDMAN

"If you open children's hearts, **you open their heads.**"

Bran FERREN

Bran Ferren is Executive Vice President for Creative Technology and Research & Development at Walt Disney Imagineering. He won the 1983 Academy of Motion Picture Arts and Sciences Technical Achievement Award for his Computer-Controlled Lightning Effects System for such films as *Places in the Heart* and *Deathtrap*. In 1987, he won the Scientific and Engineering Award for the Advanced Concept Optical Printer and the Laser Synchro-Cue System for motion picture special effects and precise camera motion. Ferren wants to bring back the lost art of interactive story telling, suggesting that it can rescue our declining state of education. He suggests that not enough effort has been expended to make Web pages engaging and beautiful. He coined the term "emotional resolution" to refer to this aspect of the technology, and says there are not enough "joyful objects" on the Web. In 1997, Ferren spoke at the ACM97 Conference on "The Next Fifty Years of Computing."

"**[Intelligent computers] will profoundly affect** our businesses and

professions, our institutions and our governments, our science, our schools,

and our personal daily lives."

Jay FORRESTER

Graduating with an M.S. degree from MIT in 1945, Jay Forrester worked on a number of analog computer projects for the U.S. Navy. In 1948, when the demands of an aircraft stability analyzer appeared to outstrip the analog computing techniques of the day, Forrester began work on a digital machine, the Whirlwind I. It would advance the state of the computer art in many fundamental ways, including the development of high-speed circuits. The Whirlwind was the first "real-time" computer, made possible by Forrester's development of "coincident-current" magnetic core memory, which remained the dominant memory technology until the 1970s. He is currently involved with the System Dynamics approach to education.

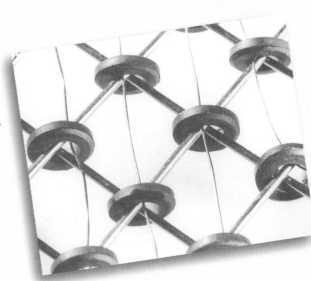

Greatly magnified section of the first core memory, used in the Whirlwind 1 computer.

**"Digital computers show the promise of
almost revolutionary contributions** to many branches of science and
engineering, as well as to the social sciences
and large-scale accounting." – JAY FORRESTER, 1948

Bob
FRANKSTON

Bob Frankston did most of the coding for *VisiCalc*, the world's
first electronic spreadsheet, after Dan Bricklin proposed the
idea. Working in his attic at night, Frankston created a working
version of the program in four weeks. Released in October
1979, the first commercial version of *VisiCalc* was 20K bytes
and available only for the Apple II computer. He holds four
degrees, all from MIT: Bachelor's degrees in mathematics and
electrical engineering (1970), an engineering degree, and a
Master's degree in electrical engineering (1974).

Bob Frankston and *VisiCalc*
co-developer Dan Bricklin on the
January, 1982 cover of Inc.

"It was fun to create something that people would use, like creating a new machine.

Once we got people to use [*VisiCalc*], **there was an interest not just in**

the programming, but in the aesthetics and usability as well."

— BOB FRANKSTON, 1986

James
GOSLING

For many years, James Gosling has designed satellite data acquisition systems, several compilers, mail systems, window managers, and the EMACS UNIX editor. He was the Lead Engineer for Sun Microsystems' Java/Hot Java project and is presently a Vice-President and Fellow at Sun. He has received a B.S. degree in computer science from the University of Calgary (1977) and a Ph.D. degree, also in computer science, from Carnegie-Mellon University (1983).

Hardware prototype machine used at Sun for developing the JAVA language.

Richard
HAMMING

Graduating with a Ph.D. degree in mathematics from the University of Illinois in 1942, Richard Hamming joined the Manhattan Project, where he was – as he describes it – the resident "Computer Janitor," translating the needs of Los Alamos National Laboratory scientists into workable computer programs. After World War II, Hamming accepted a position at Bell Telephone Laboratories and developed a means of error correction for computers that allowed for the detection and repair of single-bit errors in a data stream. He also invented a novel and widely-used statistical technique for digital filter design known as the "Hamming Window." The IEEE has instituted the Hamming Medal in his honor to recognize contributions in information science and systems.

Hamming's classic paper on "Error Detecting and Error Correcting Codes."

Error Detecting and Error Correcting Codes

By R. W. HAMMING

1. INTRODUCTION

THE author was led to the study given in this paper from a consideration of large scale computing machines in which a large number of operations must be performed without a single error in the end result. This problem of "doing things right" on a large scale is not essentially new; in a telephone central office, for example, a very large number of operations are performed while the errors leading to wrong numbers are kept well under control, though they have not been completely eliminated. This has been achieved, in part, through the use of self-checking circuits. The occasional failure that escapes routine checking is still detected by the customer and will, if it persists, result in customer complaint, while if it is transient it will produce only occasional wrong numbers. At the same time the rest of the central office functions satisfactorily. In a digital computer, on the other hand, a single failure usually means the complete failure, in the sense that if it is detected no more computing can be done until the failure is located and corrected, while if it escapes detection then it invalidates all subsequent operations of the machine. Put in other words, in a telephone central office there are a number of parallel paths which are more or less independent of each other; in a digital machine there is usually a single long path which passes through the same piece of equipment many, many times before the answer is obtained.

In transmitting information from one place to another digital machines use codes which are simply sets of symbols to which meanings or values are attached. Examples of codes which were designed to detect isolated errors are numerous; among them are the highly developed 2 out of 5 codes used extensively in common control switching systems and in the Bell Relay

1

"Once, when Sir Isaac Newton was asked how he made all of his discoveries, he replied,

'If I have seen further than others, it is by standing on the shoulders of giants.'

Today, in the programming field, we mostly stand on each other's feet."

George H. HEILMEIER

George H. Heilmeier is Bellcore's Chairman and Chief Executive Officer. He is the recipient of the John Scott Award for Scientific Achievement for his pioneering work in the development of liquid crystal displays that influenced technology development through applications in computers and consumer products. Dr. Heilmeier is a native of Philadelphia and holds a Ph.D. degree from Princeton University, as well as honorary degrees awarded by Stevens Institute of Technology and the Israel Institute of Technology (Technion). He is also the recipient of numerous awards and honors throughout his career in the computer, defense, and telecommunications industries, including the National Medal of Science in 1991. He serves on the boards of TRW, Compaq, and ADP Corporation.

Andrew R.
HELLER

Andrew R. Heller has worked in the computer industry for over thirty years, for a time serving as IBM's Director of Advanced Technology Systems. Before leaving IBM for the venture capital firm of Kleiner Perkins Caufield & Byers, he was General Manager of IBM's Independent Business Unit, responsible for that company's Unix and workstation activities. He was recently Chairman and CEO of HaL Computer Systems and is currently a consultant to the semiconductor, computer, communications, and software industries.

Gardner
HENDRIE

At Computer Controls Corporation, Hendrie designed the DDP-116, the first 16-bit minicomputer. Before IBM announced its System/360 based on the 8-bit byte, Hendrie planned to build a 14-bit machine, but then lengthened the word to 16 bits to ensure compatibility with IBMs newly "de facto" standard. A low-cost version of the DDP-116 (the 416) and a high-cost version (the 516) were developed. CCC was later purchased by Honeywell. Hendrie also designed the microNOVA, the silicon implementation of Data General's successful NOVA minicomputer. Hendrie was a founder of Stratus, where he built a hardware-based, fault-tolerant computer.

"Throughout my career as a computer designer, I have set out on explorations into the unknown. Over and over again **I undertook the design of new computers without the foggiest idea of how to do it.**"

John L.
HENNESSY

Since 1977, John L. Hennessy has been a faculty member of
Stanford University's Department of Electrical Engineering.
In 1981, he started the MIPS Project, and three years later,
he took a one-year leave of absence to found MIPS Computer
Systems. At MIPS, he refined the MIPS reduced instruction
set computer (RISC) architecture, which has since been widely
adopted by such companies as Digital Equipment Corporation,
Siemens, NEC, and Silicon Graphics, Inc. He is currently
Dean of Engineering at Stanford University.

Computer Architecture:

A Quantitative Approach,

by John L. Hennessy and

David A. Patterson

COMPUTER
ARCHITECTURE
A
QUANTITATIVE
APPROACH

JOHN L HENNESSY
&
DAVID A PATTERSON

Andy
HERTZFELD

Andy Hertzfeld became one of the principal members of the Macintosh computer design team at Apple Computer, in the 1980s, writing approximately one-third of the entire ROM code for the MAC BIOS. He left Apple in 1984 to develop Apple-compatible products such as the Thunderscan, a low-cost scanner. In 1986, he became a founding member of Radius and later a co-founder of General Magic, Inc. He earned a degree in computer science from Brown University in 1975.

The Mac Toolbox, designed by Andy Hertzfeld.

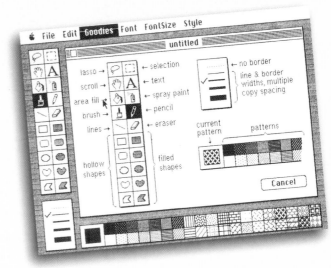

"We believe very strongly that **the user is in control** of what color something is, or what sound something has, because **every user is different,** and what is pleasing to one isn't pleasing to another."

Daniel
HILLIS

Daniel (Danny) Hillis was named the first Disney Fellow and is currently Vice President of Research and Development at The Walt Disney Company. He is also an Adjunct Professor at MIT, at the Media Lab. An inventor, scientist, and computer designer, Dr. Hillis pioneered the concept of parallel computers that is now the basis for most supercomputers. He co-founded Thinking Machines Corporation, which was the first company to build and market such systems successfully in the form of The Connection Machine. Hillis received a B.S. degree from MIT, during which time he also designed computer-oriented toys and games for the Milton Bradley Company. While still at college, he co-founded Terrapin, Inc., a producer of computer software for elementary schools.

Hillis is the recipient of the ACM's Grace Murray Hopper Award, among others, and is a Fellow of the ACM and the American Academy of Arts and Sciences. He holds over 40 patents, and was the subject of a BBC documentary, *The Seven Wonders of the World*, in which he describes his ideas about information and evolution.

The Connection Machine,

from Thinking Machines Corp.

Ted HOFF

inventors

Ted Hoff, an Applications Engineer at Intel in the 1970s, proposed a method of replacing the many discrete combinatorial logic ICs for Intel's BUSICOM calculator project with a single device capable of executing these same functions through software. He led the Intel team of Federico Faggin, Stan Mazor, and Masatoshi Shima, which brought this idea to fruition in the Intel 4004 microprocessor. Hoff graduated with a degree in electrical engineering from Rensselaer Polytechnic Institute.

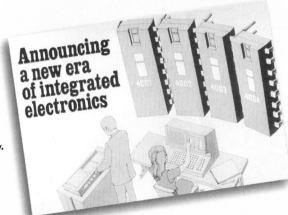

Early Intel advertisement for the 4004 microprocessor family.

Steven P. JOBS

Steven P. Jobs co-founded Apple Computer Corporation in the 1970s with Steve Wozniak. Immediately prior to founding Apple, Jobs had left Reed College and was working for Atari. He became reacquainted with his college friend, Wozniak, and the two began designing computer games as well as a telephone "blue box." They designed the Apple I computer in Jobs' family garage. The flamboyant and mercurial Jobs managed the business at Apple, supervising the introduction of many important and pioneering machines, including the Apple II and the Macintosh computers. After being ousted by John Sculley (whom Jobs had recruited to run Apple), Jobs founded the NeXT Corporation and, after that, Pixar, which was responsible for the ground-breaking, *Toy Story*, the first feature movie to be created entirely by computer animation. Jobs rejoined Apple in 1997 as a corporate consultant to help rejuvenate the company.

"Did Alexander Graham Bell do any market research
before he invented the telephone?" – ON BEING ASKED IF HE HAD CONSULTED
THE PUBLIC FOR ADVICE BEFORE DESIGNING THE MACINTOSH COMPUTER.

Robert E.
KAHN

Robert E. Kahn worked on the technical staff of the Bell Telephone Laboratories and then became Assistant Professor at MIT. During a leave of absence in the late 1960s, he consulted with Bolt, Beranek and Newman, which resulted in the system design of the first packet-switched computer network in 1971. He is, with Vint Cerf, a co-inventor of the TCP/IP Internet protocol, and has won the ACM's President's Award, as well as the ACM Software Systems Award. He is currently President, Chairman, and CEO of the Corporation for National Research Initiatives (CNRI), which provides leadership and funding for the development of the National Information Infrastructure (NII). He holds a B.E.E. degree from CUNY and M.S. and Ph.D. degrees from Princeton University.

KAY Alan

Alan Kay, a Disney Fellow and Vice President of Research and Development for the Walt Disney Company, is best known for the idea of personal computing, the concept of the intimate laptop computer, and the inventions of the now ubiquitous overlapping-window interface and modern object-oriented programming. His deep interest in children was the catalyst for these ideas, and it continues to inspire him. Kay was one of the founders of the Xerox Palo Alto Research Center (PARC), where he led one of the groups that in concert developed those ideas into modern workstations (and the forerunner of the Macintosh), the Smalltalk computer language, the overlapping-window interface, desktop publishing, the Ethernet, laser printing, and network "client servers." Kay has received many awards, including ACM's Software Systems Award and the J-D Warnier Prix D'Informatique. He is a Fellow of the American Academy of Arts and Sciences, the National Academy of Engineering, and the Royal Society of Arts. He is pictured sitting at the custom pipe organ installed in his home.

"Computers are to computing as instruments are to music.

Software is the score, whose interpretation amplifies our reach and lifts our spirit.

Leonardo da Vinci called music 'the shaping of the invisible,' and his phrase

is even more apt as a description of software."

Brian KERNIGHAN

Brian Kernighan joined Dennis Ritchie in writing *The C Programming Language* in 1978. In 1988, the American National Standards Institute (ANSI) completed a standardized version of C, "ANSI C." The second edition of *The C Programming Language* was published in the same year and described the new standard version of C. This volume has become the archetype for many style and content conventions of today's programming environment.

Leonard KLEINROCK

Leonard Kleinrock supervised the first message transmission over the Internet at UCLA in 1969, when it became the first node on the Internet. He has been called one of the "fathers" of the Internet, having developed the basic principles of packet switching a decade before the ARPAnet was deployed. He also wrote the first book on packet switching. He is a member of the National Academy of Engineering, a Guggenheim Fellow, an IEEE Fellow, and a Founding Member of the Computer Science and Telecommunications Board of the National Research Council. He has received many awards, including the 12th Marconi International Fellowship Award for pioneering work in computer networks. He received a B.S. degree in electrical engineering from the City College of New York, and M.S. and Ph.D. degrees in electrical engineering from MIT.

Donald
KNUTH

Donald Knuth is perhaps best known for having written the classic, multi-volume series, *The Art of Computer Programming*, the "Bible" of computer science pedagogy. He has written dozens of books and hundreds of articles on mathematics and computer science, and has influenced the thinking of countless students of computer science. He also invented the typesetting language $T_{e}X$ (pronounced "tech," using the ch sound from "loch"), which remains a worldwide standard for technical publishing. In *The Art of Computer Programming*, Knuth wryly compares a computer program to a recipe by quoting from *McCall's Cookbook*. He received his Ph.D. degree in mathematics from Caltech in 1963.

Surreal Numbers, one of
Donald Knuth's many books.

"I am now a happy man." – DONALD KNUTH,

AFTER GIVING UP THE USE OF EMAIL IN 1990.

inventors

Thomas
KURTZ

Tom Kurtz and John Kemeny (shown in painting at right) co-invented the BASIC computer language, which ran for the first time in May 1964 at Dartmouth College in Hanover, New Hampshire. He and Kemeny were both inspired by John McCarthy's idea that time-sharing could be used to give computer access to all the students on campus. Kurtz earned a Ph.D. degree in mathematics and statistics from Princeton University in 1956, and three years later became the first director of Dartmouth College's Computing Center. He has won several awards, including the AFIPS Pioneer Award and the IEEE Computer Science Pioneer Award.

BASIC Instructional Manual, 1964,

the first published book on BASIC.

Butler
LAMPSON

Butler Lampson has influenced the design of computer architecture, local-area networks, the raster printer, page description languages, and operating systems, and was one of the designers of the Xerox Palo Alto Research Center (PARC) Alto computer. His seminal contributions have inspired a generation of programmers. In 1967, he received a Ph.D. degree in electrical engineering and computer science from the University of California, Berkeley.

XEROX Palo Alto Research Center (PARC) Alto computer, 1973. The Alto embodied a unique combination of developments taking place at PARC and became the first system to incorporate a graphical user interface (GUI), a mouse, built-in networking, and a bit-mapped display, all in one cabinet.

J. Halcombe
LANING JR.

J. Halcombe (Hal) Laning, Jr. joined MIT's Draper Laboratory in 1945 and held a number of positions there until his retirement in 1989. He did much pioneering work in both computer science and missile guidance, including developing the first algebraic compiler, nicknamed "George," in 1952, and conceiving the theoretical development of the Q-guidance system used in the Thor and Polaris missiles in 1957. He also helped design the Apollo guidance computer and co-authored *Random Processes in Automatic Control*, an important early engineering textbook in stochastic processes. He has made many contributions in the fields of inertial guidance, computer-aided mechanical design, and the automation of automotive manufacturing processes. He received an S.B. degree in chemical engineering and a Ph.D. degree in applied mathematics from MIT. He is a member of the National Academy of Engineering and many other professional societies.

inventors

John
LASSETER

Trained in classic animation at Disney Studios, John Lasseter subsequently moved to Pixar, where he quickly mastered the techniques of computer-generated animation. His collaboration with Alvy Ray Smith, Ed Catmull, and Loren Carpenter led Pixar to develop award-winning short subjects, starting with *Andy and Wally Bee*, *Tin Toy*, and, in 1996, the feature-length *Toy Story*. Lasseter and his Pixar team received an Oscar™ for *Toy Story* in 1996.

Still frame from *Tin Toy*, a short animated film produced by Pixar's Animation Production Group, and the first computer animated film ever to receive an Academy Award™ (for Best Short Animated Film).

Robert
LUCKY

Robert Lucky is Vice President of applied research at Bellcore, the research arm of the regional Bell operating companies. He oversees applied research in network technology, architectures and services, and information sciences and services. Prior to joining Bellcore, he was Executive Director of the communications sciences research division at AT&T Bell Laboratories, where he led research into methods and technologies for future communications systems. At Bell Labs he invented the adaptive equalizer, a technique for correcting distortion in telephone signals still used in all high-speed data transmission today. He wrote *Silicon Dreams*, which discusses the ways humans and computers deal with information. He is a member of the National Academy of Engineering, and won the 1987 Marconi Prize for his contributions to data communications. He received B.S., M.S., and Ph.D. degrees in electrical engineering from Purdue University.

Benoit MANDELBROT

Benoit Mandelbrot is the inventor of fractal geometry, a system of mathematics that unifies a vast range of natural phenomena as diverse as the shape of coastlines, cloud formations, and the growth of plants. Now an IBM Fellow, Mandelbrot has held a variety of professorships. Fractals are used extensively in computer graphics and animation because they offer a mathematical method that describes many naturally occurring processes and forms. Mandelbrot earned his Ph.D. degree in mathematics at the University of Paris.

A fractal image.

Paul MARITZ

Paul Maritz is Group Vice President, Platforms and Applications, at Microsoft Corporation. He oversees the divisions contributing to Windows, Internet system software, consumer productivity software, tools, database and communications products, and evangelism activities. Since joining Microsoft Corporation in 1986, Maritz has managed various systems software product groups, including Microsoft Corporation's Networking and Windows units. Prior to joining Microsoft, Maritz spent five years at Intel Corporation. He has also worked for Burroughs Corporation and at the University of St. Andrews in Scotland. He is a graduate of the University of Cape Town and of the University of Natal, South Africa, where he studied computer science and mathematics.

Max V. MATTHEWS

Music synthesis has its origins in Music III, a programming language developed in 1960 by Max V. Matthews and his colleagues at Bell Telephone Laboratories. Music III was built on the idea of unit generators. Instruments are built by combining and connecting unit generators in an orchestra or instrument file. Note lists and other changing parameters are stored in a score file. These files are then compiled together to produce a sound file.

"Sampling a Waveform," from Max Matthews'

The Technology of Computer Music.

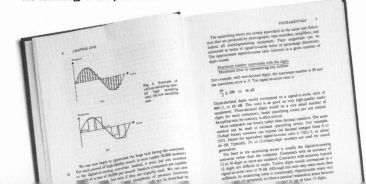

John
McCARTHY

John McCarthy created the LISP programming system while at MIT, where he and Marvin Minsky organized and directed the Artificial Intelligence Project. He also developed the concept of time-sharing in the late 1950s. McCarthy became interested in artificial intelligence while studying at Princeton University, in particular, the formalization of common sense knowledge. He earned a B.S. degree in mathematics from Caltech and a Ph.D. degree in mathematics from Princeton. In 1971, he received the ACM Turing Award. He is a member of the National Academy of Engineering and the National Academy of Science.

LISP I

PROGRAMMER'S MANUAL

March 1, 1960

John McCarthy's classic 1960

"LISP I Programmer's Manual."

Carver MEAD

Carver Mead is perhaps best known for his now-classic text *Introduction to VLSI Systems Design*, which he co-authored with Lynn Conway, and which proposed design rules for developing complex, high-density integrated circuits. His current focus is on modeling and constructing electronic versions of human biological structures – what he calls "neuromorphic electronic systems." An example of these systems is the touchpad he co-developed with Federico Faggin at Synaptics. Mead graduated from Caltech with B.S., M.S., and Ph.D. degrees in electrical engineering.

Introduction to VLSI Systems Design. Mead wrote this book with co-author Lynn Conway because he felt that few engineers designing integrated circuits knew much about computer science concepts, a problem he determined was leading to inefficient computing machines. The book became a classic and was widely influential in engineering programs across the country.

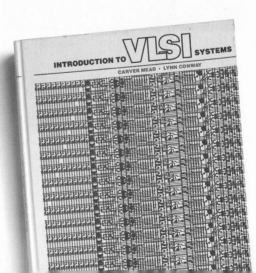

"Digital systems look like the whole world to us today.

I look on them as the start in a range of computing systems."

Robert METCALFE

Robert Metcalfe received a Ph.D. degree in computer science from MIT. His thesis, *Packet Communication*, described packet switching in the ARPAnet and Alohanet. At the Xerox Palo Alto Research Center (PARC), he was the principal inventor of Ethernet, the local-area networking technology for which he shares four patents. In 1979, Metcalfe founded 3Com Corporation and worked to promote local-area networks, particularly Ethernet. He writes a regular column for *InfoWorld*. In 1997, he served as Chair of the ACM97 Conference on "The Next Fifty Years of Computing."

An early Ethernet connector.

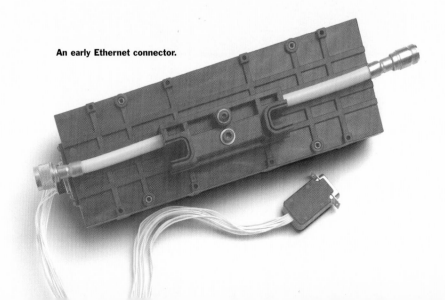

"The value of a network can be measured by the square of its users — or, more simply, **connected computers are better."** — METCALFE'S LAW

Marvin
MINSKY

Marvin Minsky has been a faculty member of MIT since 1958
and co-founder of the Artificial Intelligence Laboratory, and
has made important contributions to the fields of artificial
intelligence, cognitive psychology, mathematics, computational
linguistics, robotics, and optics. In recent years, he has worked
chiefly on imparting to machines the human capacity for
commonsense reasoning; his ideas about the mind are presented
in *The Society of Mind* (1987), also the title of the course he
teaches at MIT. He is the Toshiba Professor of Media Arts and
Sciences and Professor of Computer Science and Engineering at
MIT. Among the honors he has received are the ACM Turing
Award (1970), MIT's Killian Award (1989), the Japan Prize
(1990), and the IJCAI Research Excellence Award (1991).

The Society of Mind, by Marvin Minsky,
is about how intelligence can be
understood in times of interactive
agents.

"Our minds contain processes that enable us to solve problems we consider difficult. **'Intelligence' is our name for whichever of those processes we don't yet understand."**

Ray
OZZIE

Ray Ozzie is the Founder and President of Iris Associates, the developer of Lotus Notes software. Prior to that, at Lotus, he was the lead architect and developer of Symphony and also held positions at Software Arts, Inc., and Data General Corporation. Ozzie was named "Person of the Year" by *PC Magazine* in 1995, and has also been recognized for his contributions in the commercial application of cryptography. He also served on the National Academy of Science's National Research Council studying cryptograph issues.

"Money is not the issue. **It's how well-focused you can keep your [software] development team** and how well they can execute as the product gets bigger and bigger. Once you're successful . . . you get unbelievable numbers of customer requirements, and you try to satisfy them and still innovate a little."

Seymour PAPERT

Seymour Papert is a mathematician and one of the early pioneers of artificial intelligence. He is Director of the MIT Media Laboratory's Learning and Epistemology Group, and teaches courses on the role of computational and communications technologies in the learning process. He is renowned for his work in creating innovative computer tools for children, including the Logo computer language. He came to MIT in 1963 as Research Associate in the Electrical Engineering Department, and, before assuming his present duties, was Co-Director of the Artificial Intelligence Laboratory, Director of the Logo Group, and Professor of Mathematics and Education in the Department of Arts and Media. He wrote the influential book, *Mindstorms*. Marvin Minsky has called him "the greatest of all living education theorists. He puts into the hands of the child new conceptual tools and thus changes the learning experience from a matter of discipline and suffering into one of excitement."

Children work on the Lego Logo project at The Computer Museum's Computer Clubhouse.

"Some of the most crucial steps in mental growth are based not simply on acquiring new skills, but on **acquiring new administrative ways to use what one already knows.**" — "PAPERT'S PRINCIPLE"

David
PATTERSON

After receiving his Ph.D. degree from the University of
California, Berkeley, in 1977, David Patterson joined the
faculty, where he taught computer architecture and led the
design and implementation of RISC I (reduced instruction set
computer). This became the foundation for the popular sparc
architecture used by Fujitsu, Sun Microsystems, and Xerox.
Patterson also led the team that conceived and constructed the
first RAID system (redundant array of inexpensive disks), a
technology now used extensively in client-server computing.

John
PIERCE

John Pierce began working for Bell Telephone Laboratories in the 1930s and became Director of Communications Principles. Pierce has made many important contributions to the field of communications engineering, specifically in the area of signals and noise and in the theory of transmission channels. The author of dozens of technical articles and several important books on electronics, Pierce has written on a variety of topics for lay audiences, including music, most notably for *Scientific American* and *Atlantic Monthly*. He won the National Medal of Science in 1963. He received a Ph.D. degree from Caltech.

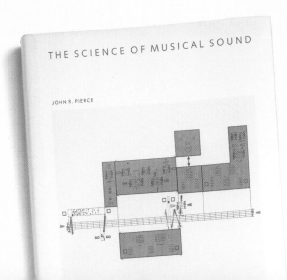

John Pierce's book on *The Science of Musical Sound*.

Rick
RASHID

After developing the MACH Operating System at Carnegie-Mellon University, Rick Rashid went on to form Microsoft Research Corp., where he is Vice President for Research. He began his career in computing in the mid-1970s working with some of the earliest workstations and local-area networks, on the threshold of the personal computing revolution.

inventors

"The challenge of the 1970s was to create a computing paradigm which allowed

a large category of skilled professionals to make effective use of dedicated computers.

Today the challenge is to build an infrastructure of software and computing

devices that will be **accessible to everyone in our society.**"

Justin R. RATTNER

Justin R. Rattner is an Intel Fellow and Director of Intel's Server Architecture Laboratory. His current R&D activities focus on future server technologies and standards. He was featured as Person of the Week by ABC World News in December, 1996 for his pioneering work on the Department of Energy ASCI Red System, the first computer to achieve sustained performance of one trillion scientific calculations per second. In 1989, he was named Scientist of the Year by *R&D* Magazine for his leadership in parallel and distributed computer architecture. He joined Intel in 1973 and became its first Principal Engineer in 1979 and a corporate Fellow in 1988. Prior to joining Intel, He held positions with Hewlett-Packard Company and Xerox Corporation. He received a B.S. degree in electrical engineering and an M.S. degree in computer science from Cornell University.

Raj
REDDY

Raj Reddy is Herbert A. Simon University Professor and Dean of the School of Computer Science at Carnegie-Mellon University. Before that he served as Director of the Robotics Institute from 1979 to 1992. His areas of interest include human-computer interaction, artificial intelligence, and rapid prototyping in manufacturing. Current active research projects include speech recognition and understanding systems, multi-media presentation technologies, collaborative writing, design, and planning, and the Automated Machine Shop project. In 1995, Reddy received the ACM Turing Award.

Dennis
RITCHIE

Dennis Ritchie is best known as the author of *The C Programming Language* and as part of the famous team of Ritchie and (Ken) Thompson. Together, they formed the driving creative force behind Bell Telephone Laboratories' legendary computer science operating group. In 1969, they created Unix, an open operating system for minicomputers. Unix helped users with general computing, word processing, and networking, and soon became a standard language. Ritchie also co-wrote Plan 9, the next-generation operating system created as the natural descendant of Unix by Thompson and Bell Labs colleague Rob Pike. Interestingly, Ritchie's favorite computer language is Alef.

Ronald L. RIVEST

Ronald L. Rivest is, with Adi Shamir and Len Adleman, one of the co-inventors of the "RSA" public-key cryptosystem, and is one of the founders of RSA Data Security. In 1977, the three men began discussing ways to make a practical public-key system. The idea for the RSA algorithm came to Rivest one night when he was suffering from a headache. The resulting algorithm is a practical public-key cipher for both confidentiality and digital signatures, based on the difficulty of factoring large numbers. He is the Edwin Webster Professor of Electrical Engineering and Computer Science at MIT, an Associate Director of MIT's Laboratory for Computer Science, and a leader of the laboratory's Cryptography and Information Security Research Group.

The classic paper, "On Digital Signatures and Public-Key Cryptography," by Ronald L. Rivest, Adi Shamir, and Len Adleman.

On Digital Signatures and Public-Key Cryptosystems
by R. L. Rivest, A. Shamir, and L. Adleman
MIT Laboratory for Computer Science
Cambridge, Mass. 02139
April 4, 1977 (Revised April 21, 1977)

The operation of raising a number to a fixed power modulo a composite modulus is shown to be sufficient to implement "digital signatures": a way of creating for a (digitized) document a recognizable, unforgeable, document-dependent, digitized signature whose authenticity the signer can not later deny. This scheme has obvious applications in the design of "electronic funds transfer" systems or "electronic mail" systems, since here the messages must be digitized in order to be transmitted.

I. Introduction

Our approach is to provide an implementation of a "public-key cryptosystem", an elegant concept invented by Diffie and Hellman [2]. Such a system provides digital signatures, as well as enabling enciphered communication between arbitrary pairs of people, without the necessity of agreeing on an enciphering key beforehand.

In a public-key cryptosystem each user A places in a public file an enciphering algorithm (or key) E_A. User A keeps to himself the details of the corresponding deciphering algorithm D_A which satisfies the equation

$$D_A(E_A(M)) = M , \text{ for any message } M. \qquad (1)$$

Both E_A and D_A must be efficiently computable. It is assumed that A does not compromise D_A when revealing E_A. That is, it should not be computationally feasible for an "enemy" to find an efficient way of computing D_A, given only a specification of the enciphering algorithm E_A. (Clearly a very inefficient way exists: to compute $D_A(C)$ just enumerate all possible messages M until one such that $E_A(M) = C$ is found. Then $D_A(C) = M$.) Only A will be able to compute D_A efficiently.

Whenever another user (say B) wishes to send A the enciphered message looks up E_A in the public file and then sends A by computing $D_A(E_A(M))=M$. By our $E_A(M)$. User A deciphers the message by computing $E_A(M)$ sent to him. If A assumptions only user A can decipher the message $E_A(M)$ it using E_B, also send a response to B he of course enciphers between A and B Therefore no transactions by the ... The only "setup" required ...

Lawrence G. ROBERTS

Lawrence G. Roberts designed and developed the ARPAnet, the predecessor to the Internet. After co-developing packet switching, Roberts founded the world's first packet data communications carrier, Telenet, which was sold to GTE in 1979 and which subsequently became the data division of Sprint. In 1982, Roberts became President and CEO of DHL Corporation. Roberts is currently President of ATM Systems, an Ethernet switching equipment manufacturer. He holds B.S., M.S., and Ph.D. degrees from MIT.

Edward H.
SHORTLIFFE

Edward H. (Ted) Shortliffe developed the MYCIN software program at Stanford University during the 1970s. One of the first rule-based expert systems, it helped doctors choose the right treatment for meningitis and bacterial infections of the blood. He is a member of the Institute of Medicine at the National Academy of Sciences and is a Fellow of the American College of Medical Informatics and the American Association for Artificial Intelligence. He has served on the Computer Science and Telecommunications Board of the National Research Council. He is Associate Dean for Information Resources and Technology, Professor of Medicine, and Professor of Computer Science at Stanford University School of Medicine.

Herbert SIMON

Herbert Simon has done research in a variety of fields, including computer science, psychology, administration, and economics, based on his interest in the human decision-making and problem-solving processes. With Allan Newell, he created GPS (General Problem Solver), a thought-provoking and controversial early artificial intelligence program. He has held research and faculty positions at the University of Chicago, the University of California, Berkeley, Carnegie-Mellon University, and other institutions. He has received the Alfred Nobel Memorial Prize in Economic Sciences and the National Medal of Science. He emigrated from Denmark in 1968 to study at the University of California, Berkeley, where he received a B.S. degree in computer science in 1972. He earned a Ph.D. degree, also in computer science, from Stanford University in 1977.

Charles SIMONYI

At the Xerox Palo Alto Research Center (PARC) during the 1970s, Charles Simonyi led a team of programmers in developing Bravo, the first WYSIWYG ("what you see is what you get") word processor. Simonyi is now Chief Architect of Microsoft Corporation. He received a B.S. degree from the University of California, Berkeley, and a Ph.D. degree from Stanford University. Prior to his schoolwork, he worked as a programmer and architect on a variety of important computers, including the ILLIAC IV. He began working at Microsoft in the early 1980s as Director of the Application Software Group, managing the creation of Multiplan, MS Word, and Excel.

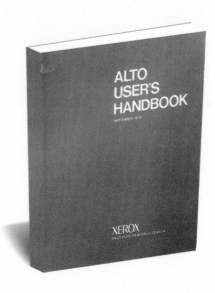

The Alto User's Handbook, which contained the documentation for BRAVO, the first "WYSIWIG" (what you see is what you get) word processor.

Larry
SMARR

Larry Smarr, a pioneer in supercomputer development, is Director of the National Center for Supercomputing Applications and Professor of Physics and Astrophysics at the University of Illinois at Urbana-Champaign. He is a Fellow of the American Academy of Arts and Sciences and of the American Physical Society, and a member of the National Academy of Engineering.

"I think that we're at a real **turning point in the computer industry.**

Microprocessor supercomputers are now emerging as major players."

Alvy Ray
SMITH

Alvy Ray Smith is the first Graphics Fellow at Microsoft Research Corp. He was the Executive Vice President and co-founder of Pixar and the Director of Computer Graphics Research at the Computer Division of Lucasfilm Ltd, where he directed the first use of full computer graphics in a successful major motion picture, *Star Trek II: The Wrath of Khan* (the "Genesis Demo"). He was co-awarded the Computer Graphics Achievement Award by the ACM's SIGGRAPH (Special Interest Group on Graphics) in 1990 for "seminal contributions to computer paint systems." Smith hired John Lasseter, Disney-trained animator, while at Pixar. The team he formed proceeded, under Lasseter as artistic director at Pixar, to create *Tin Toy*, the first computer animation to win an Academy Award,™ and *Toy Story*, the first completely computer-generated film.

Richard
STALLMAN

Richard Stallman simultaneously earned a magna cum laude degree in physics from Harvard University and served as a system programmer for Russell Nofsker's Artificial Intelligence Lab at MIT. Stallman's guiding principle was "The Hacker Ethic," the philosophy that software should be distributed for free. He worked on the development of EMACS, an editing program allowing limitless customization by users. Stallman, a "lone ranger" for "The Hacker Ethic," was awarded a MacArthur Fellowship to stay at MIT and to continue programming.

Gary STARKWEATHER

Gary Starkweather designed the first laser printer engine (codename: Dover) at the Xerox Palo Alto Research Center (PARC) – a system still used in today's laser printers. Starkweather holds twenty-nine patents relating to optics and nonimpact printing. He also received many technical awards related to optical engineering and laser technologies. In 1995, Starkweather won an Academy Award™ for his technical contributions to computer-generated film animation, while serving as a consultant for Pixar. He is a Microsoft Fellow.

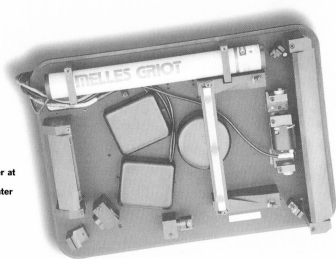

The first laserprinter engine, developed by Gary Starkweather at Xerox's Palo Alto Research Center (PARC) in the 1970s.

Michael STONEBREAKER

Michael Stonebreaker has been called the "father of object-relational technology." He is the Chief Technology Officer of Informix Software, Inc. In the 1980s, Stonebreaker was a Professor at the University of California, Berkeley, where he led a team that developed Postgres, a public-domain object-relational database. He also founded Illustra Information Technologies in 1992.

Michael Stonebreaker's classic paper,

"The Design of the Postgres Storage System."

THE DESIGN OF THE POSTGRES STORAGE SYSTEM

Michael Stonebreaker

EECS Department
University of California
Berkeley, Ca., 94720

Abstract
This paper presents the design of the storage system for the POSTGRES data base system under construction at Berkeley. It is novel in several ways. First, the storage manager supports transaction management but does so without using a conventional write ahead log (WAL). In fact, there is no code to run at recovery time, and consequently recovery from crashes is essentially instantaneous. Second, the storage manager allows a user to optionally keep the entire past history of data base objects by closely integrating an archival storage system to which historical records are spooled. Lastly, the storage manager is consciously constructed as a collection of asynchronous processes. Hence, a large monolithic body of code is avoided and opportunities for parallelism can be exploited. The paper concludes with an analysis of the storage system which suggests that it is performance competitive with WAL systems in many situations.

1. INTRODUCTION

The POSTGRES storage manager is the collection of modules that provide transaction management and access to data base objects. The design of these modules was guided by three goals which are discussed in turn below. The first goal was to provide transaction management without the necessity of writing a large amount of specialized crash recovery code. Such code is hard to debug, hard to write and must be error free. If it fails on an important client of the data manager, front page news is often the result because the client cannot access his data base and his business will be adversely affected. To achieve this goal, POSTGRES has adopted a novel storage system in which no data is ever overwritten; rather all updates are turned into insertions.

The second goal of the storage manager is to accomodate the historical state of the data base on a write-once-read-many (WORM) optical disk (or other archival medium) in addition to the current state on an ordinary magnetic disk. Consequently, we have designed an asynchronous process, called the vacuum cleaner

This research was sponsored by the Navy Electronics Systems Command under con-

William D.
STRECKER

William D. Strecker led the development of Digital Equipment Corporation's VAX architecture and played a key role in the development of the Systems Communications Architecture and Digital's Ethernet and Local Area Transport (LAT) strategies for local-area networks. He is Vice President and Chief Technical Officer at Digital, heading the Corporate Strategy and Technology Group. Strecker joined Digital in 1972 to work on cache memories and system simulation, which led to the development of the PDP-11/70. He is a Fellow of the ACM and the recipient of the IEEE Computer Society's W. W. McDowell Award in 1985 for outstanding contributions to the computer art. He has been inducted into the National Academy of Engineering.

"When I talked to customers 10 years ago about innovation, they wanted

to know every bit and byte, how it worked and why it worked. . .

Now they want to hear why it's going to make their life easy."

Bjarne
STROUSTRUP

Bjarne Stroustrup is the designer of the C++ software language and the author of *The C++ Programming Language* and *The Design and Evolution of C++*. His research interests include distributed systems, operating systems, simulation, design, and programming. He is the head of AT&T Labs' Large-scale Programming Research Department and is an AT&T Laboratories Fellow. He is actively involved in the ANSI/ISO standardization of C++. Stroustrup is the recipient of the 1993 ACM Grace Murray Hopper award and an ACM fellow. His non-research interests include general history, light literature, and music. He received a Ph.D. degree in computer science from Cambridge University, England.

"C makes it easy to shoot yourself in the foot.
**C++ makes it more difficult, but when you do
you blow your whole leg off.**"

Ivan SUTHERLAND

Ivan Sutherland's 1963 dissertation, *Sketchpad: A Man-Machine Graphical Communication System*, is one of the starting points of computer graphics. Teaching at Harvard University, he experimented with three-dimensional computer graphics, building a head-mounted graphics display in 1966 (a forerunner of today's virtual reality systems). In 1968, he co-founded Evans & Sutherland, a computer graphics company. Holder of twelve patents, Sutherland is now a Vice-President and a Fellow at Sun Microsystems, Inc. He graduated with a Ph.D. degree in electrical engineering from MIT in 1963.

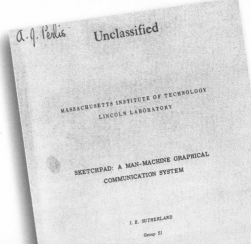

Ivan Sutherland's landmark 1963 paper, "Sketchpad: A Man-Machine Graphical Communication System."

Ken
THOMPSON

Ken Thompson co-invented the Unix operating system with Dennis Ritchie at Bell Telephone Laboratories. It was a scaled-down version of the Multics operating system, hence the pun in the name "Unix." Thanks to the development of the C programming language by Ritchie, Unix became portable over many computer platforms. He received B.S. and M.S. degrees from the University of California, Berkeley. He is an amateur pilot, and once traveled to Moscow to fly a MiG-29.

"**Computing is an addiction.** Electronics is a similar addiction, but not as clean. Much dirtier. Things burn out."

Joseph TRAUB

Starting in 1959, Joseph Traub pioneered research in what is now called information-based complexity, or the "thermodynamics" of computation. His current work ranges from new fast methods for pricing financial derivatives to investigating what is scientifically knowable. He has written eight books and is Founding Editor of the *Journal of Complexity*. He has received many honors, and has been elected to the National Academy of Engineering. Traub is the Edwin Howard Armstrong Professor of Computer Science at Columbia University and External Professor at the Santa Fe Institute in New Mexico.

Steve WOZNIAK

Steve Wozniak (Woz) built his first computer when he was 13 years old. At 19, he met 14-year-old Steve Jobs. The two teenagers built an electronic "blue box" enabling them to make toll-free calls by seizing telephone company lines. A member of the Homebrew Computer Club, Wozniak's involvement resulted in the Apple I design. In 1976, with orders for 50 machines from the Byte Shop in Mountain View, California, Apple Computer, Inc., was born. The Apple I used a MOS 6502 CPU and came with 8K of RAM. It cost $666, and only about 220 were produced. Wozniak has returned to Apple Computer as a consultant. He also teaches computing in his home community of Los Gatos, California, and is an advocate for educating future generations about computing.

The Apple II computer, one of the most popular and influential of the early personal computers.

Entrepreneurs

The entrepreneur has always been someone who knows something before anyone else, and is able to act on it first. In the world of high tech, by contrast, the entrepreneur is someone who knows something ten seconds before anyone else, and can act on it five seconds before anyone else. Today's computer entrepreneurs develop products not in normal years, but in "Internet Years," a fanciful term (Einstein would have loved it) for product development cycles that take months instead of years, and that keep entrepreneurs on their toes more often than ballet dancers. Today's computer users have barely installed version 1.0 of their software when version 2.0 appears, and are astounded by the dizzying hardware price wars the industry is so fond of. For the entrepreneur, the entire development process often represents what an industry wag once called a series of "insurmountable opportunities." But that's just the sort of challenge the people in this chapter love to set themselves.

193

Joseph
ALSOP

Joseph Alsop is President and CEO of Progress Software Corporation, a supplier of application development tools for open and client/server computing. He began his career at MIT as a researcher for project MAC, which was then the principal organization within MIT devoted to research in computer science. He is the brother of Stewart Alsop. He received a B.S.E.E. degree from MIT, and also did graduate work at the Sloane School of Management.

Gene
AMDAHL

During the 1960s, Gene Amdahl was Director of IBM's Advanced Computing Systems Laboratory in Menlo Park, California, where he led the design of the IBM/360 computer and other models, working with Project Manager Fred Brooks, Jr. In 1970, he left IBM to found the Amdahl Corporation, where he remained until 1980. He has also served as Chairman of Trilogy Systems, which develops high-performance computer systems. Amdahl has won many awards, including the ACM/ IEEE Eckert-Mauchly Award. He is a Fellow of the National Academy of Engineering and the IEEE, and a distinguished Fellow of the British Computer Society. He received a B.S.E.P. degree from South Dakota State University, and M.S. and Ph.D. degrees in theoretical physics from the University of Wisconsin.

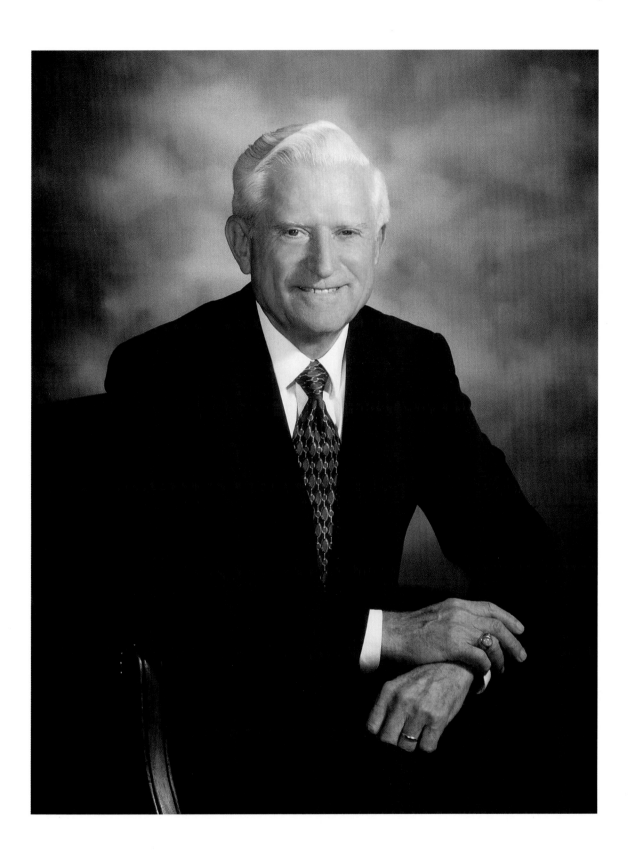

Carol BARTZ

Carol Bartz is Chairman and CEO of Autodesk, Inc., a supplier of design software, including *AutoCad*. Prior to AutoDesk, she held positions at Sun Microsystems, Digital Equipment Corporation, and 3M Corporation. She has a B.S. degree in computer science from the University of Wisconsin and has received an honorary D.S. degree from Worcester Polytechnic Institute. She has also won the Donald C. Burnham Manufacturing Management Award from the Society of Manufacturing Engineers. Within months of taking on the AutoDesk assignment, Bartz was diagnosed with breast cancer, which she conquered while also raising a family.

Eric
BENHAMOU

Eric Benhamou is Chairman and CEO of 3Com Corporation.
Benhamou co-founded Bridge Communications, an early
pioneer in connecting terminals to host mainframes. Prior
to that he spent four years at Zilog, and also chaired the
American Electronics Association's National Information
Infrastructure Task Force. *Communications Week* magazine
named him an Industry Visionary, and he has received the
President's Environment and Conservation Challenge Award.
He holds an M.S. degree in electrical engineering from
Stanford University.

Jeff BEZOS

Jeff Bezos is the founder and CEO of Amazon.com Books, which offers over one million titles via its web site. After graduating from Princeton summa cum laude, Phi Beta Kappa, in electrical engineering and computer science in 1986, Bezos joined FITEL, a high-tech start-up company in New York. In 1988, he joined Bankers Trust Company, New York, leading the development of computer systems that helped manage $250+ billion in assets and becoming their youngest VP in February 1990. From 1990 to 1994, Bezos helped build a technically sophisticated quantitative hedge fund on Wall Street for D. E. Shaw and Company, New York, becoming their youngest Senior Vice President in 1992.

"The very best way to promote oneself online is by word of mouth. This is because one person can tell 5000 people something as easily as he can tell five people."

Jeff
BRAUN

Jeff Braun is Senior Vice President, Studio Development at Electronic Arts, which acquired Maxis in 1997. Prior to that, he was Chairman and CEO of Maxis, where he developed and marketed the SimCity game, first introduced in 1989. SimCity belongs to the software genre he calls "software toys." Maxis develops software for the home-creativity and children's markets as well as the school market, featuring reality-based simulations to help children learn through hands-on experience. The company is now part of Electronic Arts. Braun was named one of the "Net's Top Fifty" by *Newsweek* magazine in 1996.

"People who use our software are more interested in **experiencing something that doesn't talk down to them or require quick reflexes.**"

entrepreneurs

Nolan
BUSHNELL

At age ten, Nolan Bushnell was a licensed ham radio operator. He received his electrical engineering degree from the University of Utah. In 1972, he and Al Alcorn devised the table-tennis-like game Pong, launching the national video-game craze. Since then he has been involved in a number of start-up companies in the areas of robotics, toys, and games. Bushnell says he "likes getting companies started, not running them." J.A.N. Lee has called him the "P. T. Barnum of Silicon Valley."

The Computer Space arcade game, developed by Nolan Bushnell prior to the successful Pong. He was inspired by playing SpaceWar! (the first interactive computer game) at the University of Utah. But the Computer Space game befuddled its intended audience in bars and was never successful. By contrast, the first version of Pong placed in a bar "broke" when its till filled up with quarters.

"**Business is the greatest game of all** – lots of complexity

and a minimum of rules. And you can keep score with money."

Rod
CANION

Rod Canion is Chairman of Insource Technology Corporation, which specializes in services for health-care organizations.
He was co-founder of Compaq Computer Corporation, which
created the first portable IBM-compatible PC. He
graduated from the University of Houston in 1966 with a B.S.
degree in electrical engineering and received his M.S. degree
in electrical engineering, with an emphasis in computer
science, in 1968. That same year, he began working for Texas
Instruments, Inc., and continued there until 1981. In 1982,
Compaq Computer Corporation was formed when Canion,
Jim Harris, and Bill Murto, two fellow TI engineers, each put
up $1000 to start the company. Canion has won many awards,
including Houston's "International Executive of the Year" and
was selected as "CEO of the Decade" in 1989 by Financial
News Net.

"The life of an entrepreneur is pretty easy . . . you have to work seven days a week, but you only have to work half a day, and **you can pick the first 12 hours or the second 12 hours."**

Doug CARLSTON

Doug Carlston is Chairman of Broderbund Software, Inc., of Novato, California. Broderbund was founded in 1982 by Carlston and his brother Gary, the sons of a theology professor from Dubuque, Iowa. (*Broderbund* comes from the Swedish and Danish words for *brothers* and the German word for *alliance*.) Broderbund's first success, in 1984, was Print Shop, one of the first desktop graphics programs for PCs. This was followed by the children's software title *Where in the World is Carmen Sandiego?* and, in 1995, *MYST*, a seminal influence on interactive games, which has sold over 500,000 copies. Doug Carlston is currently helping develop Internet and online products.

"We have a preference **for evergreen categories.** We look for opportunities to create products that will last a long time."

John
CHAMBERS

John Chambers is President and CEO of Cisco Systems, San Jose, California. He joined the company in 1991 as Senior Vice President of Worldwide Operations. Prior to Cisco, he spent eight years at Wang Laboratories, the last two as Senior Vice President of U.S. Operations. He was named one of the top 25 managers of 1996 by Business Week magazine, and one of "The Hot 25" CEOs of 1996 by CMP Media. He also received the 1996 Communications Week Industry Visionary Award. He serves on the President Clinton's Advisory Committee for Trade Policy. He received an M.B.A. degree in finance and management from Indiana University, and a J.D. degree and B.S./B.A. degree in business from West Virginia University.

"If you are not one of the first five players in with a stable product,

you are not going to become No. 1 or No. 2.

You either partner with one of those first five, or you acquire."

George
CONRADES

George Conrades is President and CEO of BBN Corporation in Cambridge, Massachusetts, a provider of Internet access and value-added services to large businesses. Conrades is the former Senior Vice President of IBM, where he ran U.S. operations and oversaw the creation of a wholly-owned subsidiary, Integrated Systems Solutions Corporation. He established IBM's Asia/Pacific Group, with headquarters in Tokyo, Japan. He has a B.A. degree in physics and mathematics from Ohio Wesleyan University and an M.B.A. degree from the University of Chicago.

Scott D. COOK

Scott D. Cook is the Co-Founder and Chairman of Intuit, Inc., developers of *Quicken*™ and other financial software. Prior to Intuit, Cook managed consulting assignments in banking and technology for Bain and Company, and, before that, worked at Proctor and Gamble. Watching his wife paying bills during the early 1980s inspired him to co-develop *Quicken* with Tim Proulx. He introduced it in 1984, applying the marketing techniques he had learned at P&G. Cook has B.A. degrees in mathematics and economics from the University of Southern California, and an M.B.A degree from Harvard University. He is on the board of Amazon.com and has an ongoing personal interest in Japanese culture.

Wilfred J. CORRIGAN

Wilfred J. Corrigan is Principal Founder and Chairman of the Board and CEO of LSI Logic Corporation, the "System on a Chip" company, which designs and produces custom semiconductors, including application-specific integrated circuits (ASICs). Prior to that, he was Chairman of Fairchild Camera and Instrument Corporation. He joined Fairchild as a Group Director in August 1968, and held a variety of management positions before becoming Chairman in May 1977. Corrigan was born in Liverpool, England, and is now a U.S. citizen.

Joseph B.
COSTELLO

Joseph B. Costello is President and CEO of Cadence
Design Systems, Inc. Prior to that, he was President
and COO of SDA Systems, Inc., one of two companies
that eventually merged to form Cadence, which develops
electronic design automation (EDA) software and
provides design service support.

Michael
DELL

Michael Dell is Chairman and CEO of Dell Computer, Inc., Austin, Texas, which he founded in 1984. Prior to Dell, and while a student at the University of Texas, he founded PCs Limited, which sold PCs and components directly to customers. It was soon generating over $50,000 of business per month. By 1997, Dell Computer had total revenues of over $1 billion – and was selling more than $1 million worth of computers per day on the Internet.

"The Internet is the **ultimate direct selling medium.**"

Lawrence J.
ELLISON

Larry Ellison is Chairman and CEO of Oracle Corporation. Ellison began his career by dropping out of the University of Illinois and going to work as a programmer in Silicon Valley for such companies as Ampex Corporation and Amdahl Corporation. In 1977, with Robert Miner, he co-founded Oracle Corporation in Redwood Shores, California, to develop relational database software. His initial investment in the company was $1,200. He was once nearly killed while bodysurfing in Hawaii, and brought Oracle back from near bankruptcy in 1990.

"I hate the PC, but I love the Internet."

Judy
ESTRIN

Judy Estrin is CEO of Precept Software, Inc., of Palo Alto, California, formed in March 1995 to develop and market video communications products for corporate Intranets. The company creates real-time multimedia applications. She began her career at Zilog, forming a team that would later found Bridge Communications. After that they managed the start-up Network Computing Devices (NCD), a maker of X terminals. She received two master's degrees in electrical engineering and computer science from Stanford University. While there, she occasionally received 3AM calls from her adviser, Vint Cerf, who wanted her to help test TCP/IP connections.

"I've learned that technology for technology's sake doesn't really matter to anyone.

What matters is how to apply technology to solve a problem.

That's become my biggest interest."

Gordon E.
EUBANKS, JR.

Gordon E. Eubanks, Jr., is President and CEO of Symantec
Corporation and a member of the Board of Directors. Prior
to that, he was Vice President of Digital Research, Inc.'s
commercial systems division. He founded Compiler Systems,
Inc., and authored its products, including CBASIC, one of
the first successful languages on personal computers. He
received a B.S. degree in electrical engineering from Oklahoma State University and an M.S. degree in computer science from Naval Postgraduate School in Monterey, California.
He is a member of the IEEE and ACM and has served as both
President and Chairman of the Board of Directors for the
Software Publishers Association.

Robert O.
EVANS

Robert O. Evans joined IBM in 1951 and convinced IBM
management to produce a software-compatible family of
computers with a wide range of performance characteristics –
the IBM System/360. The 360 family was to become the
most successful family of computers in history. He shared the
National Medal of Technology in 1985 with Erich Bloch and
Fred Brooks, Jr. Evans graduated from Iowa State University
in 1949 with a bachelor's degree in electrical engineering.

The IBM system/360, Model 44.

"The programmer builds, from pure thought-stuff, concepts and very flexible representations thereof. Because the medium is tractable, we expect few difficulties in implementation; hence our pervasive optimism. Because our ideas are faulty, we have bugs; hence our optimism is unjustified."

Robert R.
EVERETT

Robert R. Everett managed the pioneering Whirlwind
computer project at MIT's Lincoln Labs, working for Jay
Forrester. He was born in Yonkers, New York, and received a
B.S. degree in electrical engineering from Duke University in
1942. That summer, shortly after entering MIT to pursue a
master's degree, he joined the Whirlwind team. He was
instrumental in developing the fastest and most reliable
computer of its day. Everett co-founded The Computer
Museum with Ken Olsen, and was instrumental in preserving
the Whirlwind computer.

The Whirlwind 1 Test Control, taken in 1957.

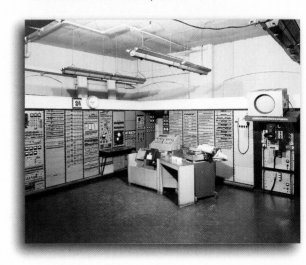

"From March 14, 1951 . . . until June 1, 1952, 2100 hours of [Whirlwind] computer time was scheduled for applications use. The machine was in successful operation for 85% of this scheduled time."

David
FILO

David Filo is co-founder and "Chief Yahoo" of Yahoo!, Inc., with Jerry Wang. In 1994, while in the Ph.D. program in electrical engineering at Stanford University, Filo and Yang co-authored the *Yahoo! Online Guide*. A year later they took a leave of absence from school to found Yahoo!, and in 1996 the company went public. In 1996, Filo, age 30, and Yang, age 28, became the youngest people to endow a chair at Stanford – the Yahoo! Founders Professor of the Stanford School of Engineering. The company pledged another $2 million of free advertising for non-profits on the Yahoo! site. Filo received a B.S. degree in computer engineering from Tulane University and an M.S. degree in electrical engineering from Stanford University.

"Stanford said '[Yahoo's] all yours. Good luck — we hope you're successful.'

I don't think a lot of schools would have done that."

William E.
FOSTER

William E. Foster is Chairman and CEO of Stratus Computer, Inc. Stratus introduced the first commercial, hardware-based fault-tolerant computer in 1982. Today the company markets middleware and applications software and related professional services. Prior to co-founding Stratus, Foster was Vice President of Software Engineering at Data General Corporation. He has a B.A. degree in mathematics from San Jose State University, and both an M.S. degree in mathematics and an M.B.A. degree from the University of Santa Clara.

Christopher B.
GALVIN

Christopher B. Galvin is President and CEO of Motorola, Inc. The son of the current Chairman of the Executive Committee, Robert Galvin, he began working part-time at Motorola in 1967 and full-time in 1973, rising through a variety of sales, marketing, and managerial positions. He went from sales and product management to the communications group, and was later a General Manager of the paging group before going on to the corporate staff in 1988. He received B.A. and M.B.A. degrees from Northwestern University.

Robert
GALVIN

Robert Galvin is Chairman of the Executive Committee at Motorola, Inc. He started his career at Motorola in 1940. The company was formed in 1928 by his father, Paul, to produce car radios for the rapidly growing automobile market. Robert Galvin led the company from 1959 until 1990. He is currently a member and past Chairman of the Board of Trustees of the Illinois Institute of Technology. He has received many honorary degrees and awards, including election to the National Business Hall of Fame and the National Medal of Technology in 1991. Motorola was the first large, company-wide winner of the Malcolm Baldridge National Quality Award, presented by President Reagan in 1988. Galvin attended the University of Notre Dame and the University of Chicago.

Lawrence L.
GARLICK

Lawrence L. Garlick is Chairman and CEO of Remedy Corporation in Mountain View, California. Remedy develops client/server software to automate internal operation processes. Prior to that, he ran the communications software group at Sun Microsystems, Inc. He consulted with Accel Partners, which later financed the start-up of Remedy in January 1991.

"There's no way to buy market share through acquisitions –
the only way to grow is to compete harder."

William H.
GATES

William H. (Bill) Gates is Chairman and CEO of Microsoft Corporation, the world's largest computer software company. He left Harvard University in 1975 after he and friend Paul Allen developed a BASIC interpreter for the newly introduced MITS Altair 8800 microcomputer. Gates wrote the program using an Altair emulator program running on Harvard's PDP-10 minicom-puter. He sent it, via paper tape, to Allen, who was visiting the MITS factory in Albuquerque, New Mexico. Allen loaded the tape, and the Teletype replied with "READY," indicating that the program was functional. Gates and Allen then formed Microsoft to continue developing software for microcomputers.

The original MITS Altair BASIC paper tape, 1975. The MITS Altair computer was introduced to the world on the cover of the January 1975 *Popular Electronics*. Bill Gates and Paul Allen saw it and were inspired to create a BASIC interpreter for it. The program fit in less than 4K of memory.

Louis V.
GERSTNER JR.

Louis V. (Lou) Gerstner, Jr., is Chairman of the Board and
CEO of the International Business Machines Corporation
(IBM). Prior to joining IBM, Gerstner served for four years
as Chairman and CEO of RJR Nabisco, Inc. This followed an
eleven-year career at American Express Company, where he
was President of the parent company and Chairman and
CEO of its largest subsidiary, American Express Travel Related
Services Company. Before that he was a Director of the
management consulting firm of McKinsey & Company, Inc.
He received a bachelor's degree from Dartmouth College and
an M.B.A. degree from Harvard Business School. He has won
many awards for his work in education, including the
Cleveland E. Dodge Medal for Distinguished Service to
Education from Teachers College, Columbia University.

Charles M.
GESCHKE

Charles M. Geschke co-founded Adobe Systems in 1982 with John Warnock. He was principal scientist at the Xerox Palo Alto Research Center (PARC) Computer Sciences Lab, where he formed the Imaging Sciences Laboratory in 1980. At PARC, he directed research activities in computer science, graphics, optics, and image processing. He received a B.A. degree in classics and an M.S. degree in mathematics from Xavier University. He received a Ph.D. degree in computer science from Carnegie-Mellon University in 1972.

Andrew S.
GROVE

Andrew S. (Andy) Grove is President and CEO of Intel
Corporation. Prior to Intel, he was Assistant Director of
Research and Development at Fairchild Semiconductor's
R&D Labs in the 1960s. He has received many awards,
including the 1987 Engineering Leadership Recognition
Award and the AEA Medal of Achievement. He is a Fellow of
the Academy of Arts and Sciences, and author of "Grove's
Law," which states that "telecommunications bandwidth
doubles every hundred years," an indication of how slowly
the telecommunications industry is growing in comparison to
the computer industry. He received a B.S. degree in chemical
engineering from the City College of New York and a Ph.D.
degree from the University of California, Berkeley.

"The revolution started twenty five years ago with a small sliver of silicon known as the microprocessor . . . I believe we are only at the beginning of this revolution in progress, and **the best in personal computing is yet to come.**"

William
HEWLETT

In 1939, William Hewlett co-founded the Hewlett-Packard Company
with Stanford University friend David Packard, and built an audio
oscillator, the company's first product. Hewlett-Packard's first business
address was in a garage in Palo Alto, California. He was President of
Hewlett-Packard until 1977. Over four decades, he has served as
spokesman for many electronics industry bodies, and received the
National Medal of Science in 1985. He earned two bachelor's degrees
at Stanford University in arts and engineering, and received a master's
degree in electrical engineering from MIT in 1939.

David Packard co-founded the Hewlett-Packard Corporation with
his friend and fellow Stanford alumnus William R. Hewlett in 1939,
serving as President and later Chairman until his death in 1996.
The two partners pooled a total of $538 to launch the new company.
Packard left the company from 1969 until 1971 to become Deputy
Secretary of Defense in the first Nixon administration. He was
President and Chairman of the David and Lucille Packard Foundation,
and a director of several corporations. He received over seventy
honorary degrees and awards, and received B.S. and M.S. degrees
in electrical engineering from Stanford University.

David
PACKARD

Max
HOPPER

Max Hopper is the founder of SABRE Group, which pioneered electronic commerce for the travel industry. During his tenure, SABRE grew from serving the needs of American Airlines to becoming the world's largest computer reservations system. Hopper also served as Executive Vice President for Bank of America from 1982 through 1985. Prior to joining American Airlines in 1972, he worked for Shell Oil Company, Electronic Data Systems, and United Airlines. Hopper currently serves on the Board of Directors of Gartner Group, Inc., Legent Corporation, and Computer Language Research, Inc.

"If you want to sell a single airline seat at 100,000 terminals all over the world, you have to do that centrally."

Charles
HOUSE

Charles (Chuck) House is Vice President of Dialogic
Corporation, President and General Manager of Spectron
Microsystems in Santa Barbara, California, and President of
the Association for Computing Machinery (ACM). Prior to
that, he was at Hewlett-Packard from 1962 to 1991, serving
in several roles, including Corporate Engineering Director,
managing the Logic Systems and Software Engineering
Systems divisions. He is an IEEE Fellow for Logic State
Analysis, and has won many awards, including the Electronics
Award of Achievement and Hewlett-Packard's Chuck House
Productivity Award. He serves on the board of The Computer
Museum. House received a B.S. in Engineering Physics from
Caltech and an M.S.E.E. degree from Stanford University, an
M.A. degree in the history of science and technology from
Colorado University, and an M.B.A. degree from the Western
Behavioral Sciences Institute.

"We have a great responsibility to the world
to monitor, gauge, and guide the impact of our technologies."

David L.
HOUSE

David L. House is Chairman, President, and CEO of Bay
Networks. Before that, he spent twenty-two years at Intel
Corporation, serving in several key management, marketing,
and strategic planning roles, including Senior Vice President
of Corporate Strategy and Senior Vice President and General
Manager of Intel's Enterprise Server Group. He began his
professional career in 1965 at Raytheon, and later went on to
Honeywell's Computer Control Division, where he received
Honeywell's highest technology award, the H.W. Sweatt
Engineer Scientist Award for his definition and development of
a new computer. In 1972, he went to Microdata, and then on
to Intel in 1974. He earned a B.S. degree in electrical engineering from Michigan Technological University and an M.S.
degree in electrical engineering from Northeastern University.
He is a Trustee of The Computer Museum.

Philippe
KAHN

entrepreneurs

Philippe Kahn is CEO of Starfish Software. A native of France, Kahn studied with Niklaus Wirth, the author of Pascal. He was one of the key programmers for the first microprocessor-based personal computer, the Micral, built by Thi Truong. After coming to California, he founded Borland International, which produced a number of well-known software packages, including *Turbo-Pascal, C ++, Quattro* and *Sidekick* for amazingly low prices. Kahn enjoys jazz, martial arts and Siberian huskies.

The Micral computer, the first microprocessor-based personal computer, for which Philippe Kahn was one of the first key programmers.

"The biggest paradigm shift since the personal computer
is the rise of the Web and on-line services, and the convergence of telephones and
computers. The action is now groupware and collaborative computing using
the Web as a wide-area network."

S. Jerrold
KAPLAN

S. Jerrold (Jerry) Kaplan heads OnSale, Inc., which offers online shopping services. In 1981, Kaplan co-founded Teknowledge, now a public artificial intelligence company. He served as Principal Technologist at Lotus Development Corporation from 1985 to 1987, where he co-authored *Lotus Agenda*, the first personal information management software. In 1987, he founded GO, the hand-held, pen-based computer company that is the subject of his book, *Start Up!*. GO was later sold to AT&T. He received a B.A. degree in history and philosophy of science from the University of Chicago, and a Ph.D. degree in computer and information science from the University of Pennsylvania, where he specialized in artificial intelligence. He was a Research Associate from 1979 to 1981 in the Computer Science Department of Stanford University.

"The real question is not why [GO Corporation] died, but rather why it survived as long as it did with no meaningful sales." – FROM START-UP

Mitchell
KAPOR

Mitchell Kapor is President of Kapor Enterprises, Inc., in Cambridge, Massachusetts. He founded Lotus Development Corporation in the early 1980s, where he served as President and CEO. He developed *1-2-3*, the first major software application for the IBM PC, along with many other products, including *Symphony*. Following that he was CEO of On Technology Corporation and President and Board Member of the Electronic Frontier Foundation. He has also served as Adjunct/Visiting Professor at MIT. He received a B.A. degree in psychology from Yale University in 1971 and a master's degree in psychology from Beacon College in 1978.

"[The Internet] is one of the world's largest **functioning anarchies.**"

Mitchell
KERTZMAN

Mitchell Kertzman is the CEO and President of Sybase, Inc.,
a provider of client/server and Internet software and services.
Prior to that, he was the CEO of Powersoft Corporation,
which he founded. He has also served as the President of the
Massachusetts Software Council, President of the Boston
Latin School Foundation, and a Director of the Massachusetts
Taxpayers Foundation and the United Way of Massachusetts.
He has served on the Board of Overseers at The Computer
Museum, the Massachusetts Business Roundtable, and the
New England Advisory Council of the Federal Reserve Bank
of Boston. In 1993, he received *Inc* magazine's and Ernst &
Young's "New England Entrepreneur of the Year" award. He
served on the New York State Commission on Industrial
Competitiveness.

"Every good war has its arms merchants. **Today that role is filled by venture capitalists** . . . The nature of arms merchants is that they make money no matter who wins."

Steven T. KIRSCH

Steven T. Kirsch is Founder and Chairman of the Board of Infoseek. Prior to that, he co-founded Frame Technology Corporation, where he served as President and Chairman of the Board. He invented the optical mouse, obtained two U.S. patents on mouse technology, and founded Mouse Systems Corporation in 1982. He received B.S. and M.S. degrees in electrical engineering and computer science from MIT. In 1987, he was ranked the 17th most successful entrepreneur under age 30 in the United States by the Association of Collegiate Entrepreneurs.

David E. LIDDLE

David E. Liddle is President and CEO of Interval Research Corporation, which he co-founded with Paul Allen, the co-founder of Microsoft Corporation. Interval performs research in the areas of information, interaction, communications, and computer science. Liddle was also Founder, President, and CEO of Metaphor, Inc. Prior to that, he spent ten years at the Xerox Palo Alto Research Center (PARC) in the Information Products Group. He was responsible for developing Xerox's client/server architecture, including the Ethernet, LAN, and the Xerox Star computer, the first commercial implementation of the graphical user interface (GUI). He is Consulting Professor of Computer Science and Electrical Engineering at Stanford University.

Dan
LYNCH

Dan Lynch is Founder and Chairman of Cybercash, Inc., and the founder of Interop Company, a division of Softbank Expos. As Director of the Information Processing Division for the Information Sciences Institute in Marina del Ray, California, he led the ARPAnet team that made the transition from the original NCP protocols to the current TCP/IP-based protocols. He has an M.A. degree in mathematics from UCLA. When time permits, he plants grapes for his vineyard, Lynch Knoll, and adds to his world-class wine collection. The vineyard has a real Cray 1 supercomputer on display.

Edward R.
McCRACKEN

Edward R. McCracken is Chairman of the Board and CEO of Silicon Graphics, Inc., in Mountain View, California. Prior to joining Silicon Graphics, McCracken spent sixteen years with Hewlett-Packard in a number of senior management positions. During 1994 and 1995, he co-chaired the United States Advisory Council for the National Information Infrastructure, which advised the Clinton administration on a national strategy to accelerate development of the information superhighway. He received the U.S. National Medal of Technology in 1995, and has received numerous other honors and awards, including the "Executive of the Year" award from the National Computer Graphics Association (1989). He received a B.S. degree in electrical engineering from Iowa State University and an M.B.A. degree from Stanford University.

Scott McNEALY

Scott McNealy is Chairman, President, and CEO of Sun Microsystems, Inc., in Mountain View, California, which he co-founded in 1982 with two other 27-year-olds. He has been a champion of the JAVA language and the network computer. He serves as the Vice Chairman for Trade of the Computer Systems Policy Project, a consortium of thirteen of the largest U.S. computer companies that addresses public policy issues affecting the industry and the country. He is also on the Board of Directors of Iwerks Entertainment and the Santa Clara County Manufacturers Board. He received a B.A. degree in economics from Harvard University and an M.B.A. degree from Stanford University.

"The network is the computer."

William
MELTON

William Melton is CEO of CyberCash, Inc. which offers secure financial transactions over the Internet. In 1971, he founded Real-Share, Inc., a database and telecommunications company, followed by VeriFone, Inc., a transaction automation company. In 1991, he was the funding founder of Transaction Network Systems (TNS), a nationwide customized network for financial transactions. In addition to his continued service on the boards of both VeriFone and TNS, he is also a member of the boards of America OnLine and the Bionomics Institute. He holds a master's degree in Asian studies and Chinese philosophy.

Gordon
MOORE

Gordon Moore is the Co-Founder and Chairman of Intel Corporation. He worked with Robert Noyce at Shockley Semiconductor Laboratory, and the pair eventually founded Fairchild Semiconductor. At Fairchild, Moore worked closely with Noyce, developing his research interest in extending the capabilities of transistors. Moore was able to implement Noyce's concepts to create "wireless clusters" of transistors, the basic idea of the "chip." In 1968, Noyce and Moore founded Intel Corporation. He earned his Ph.D. degrees in chemistry and physics from Caltech.

"The number of semiconductors on a chip **doubles approximately every 18 months.**" – MOORE'S LAW

John P.
MORGRIDGE

John P. Morgridge is Chairman of Cisco Systems, Inc., supplier of internetworking products. Prior to that, he was President and CEO of GRID Systems and Vice President of Marketing, Sales, and Service for Stratus Computer. Before that he spent twenty years at Honeywell Information Systems. He has an M.B.A. degree from Stanford University and a B.B.A. degree from the University of Wisconsin.

Nathan
MYHRVOLD

Nathan Myhrvold is Chief Technology Officer and a member of the Executive Committee for Microsoft Corporation. He is responsible for the broad strategic and business planning for the entire company. Prior to that, he was President and CEO of Dynamical Systems, a Berkeley software company, and a Postdoctoral Fellow in the Department of Applied Mathematics and Theoretical Physics at Cambridge University, working with Professor Stephen Hawking on research in cosmology, quantum field theory in curved space time, and quantum theories of gravitation. Myhrvold holds a doctorate in theoretical and mathematical physics and a master's degree in mathematical economics from Princeton University, among other degrees. He has received certificates in mountain climbing, formula car racing, photography, and French cooking. He has competed twice in the world barbecue championship in Memphis, Tennessee, winning first- and second-place titles.

"The brain has no Moore's law. We're not getting smarter every year. Computers are."

Kenneth H.
OLSEN

Kenneth H. (Ken) Olsen founded Digital Equipment Corporation in 1957 and served as its President until his retirement in 1992. Before that, he was on the staff of the MIT Digital Computer Laboratory for seven years, where he led a group at MIT's Lincoln Laboratories in designing and constructing the MTC computer used in the SAGE Air Defense Computer design program. He is a member of the Board of Directors of Polaroid Corporation and the Corporation at MIT. With Robert Everett, he co-founded The Computer Museum and was its first Chairman. He has received many awards, and was inducted into the National Inventors Hall of Fame. He also received the MCI Communications Information Technology Leadership Award for Innovation, given by the *ComputerWorld* Smithsonian awards, as well as the Founder's Medal from the IEEE and the National Medal of Technology. He received B.S. and M.S. degrees in electrical engineering from MIT.

M. Kenneth
OSHMAN

M. Kenneth Oshman is President, Chairman, and CEO of Echelon Corporation, creators of LonWorks Networks. He was one of the Founders of Rolm, whose name is made up of the initials of the four founders. He was a Director of the American Electronics Association for five years, and is a Director of Sun Microsystems, Inc. and Knight-Ridder, Inc., He is a member of the National Academy of Engineering, Phi Beta Kappa, Tau Beta Pi, and other professional organizations. He received B.A. and B.S. degrees from Rice University, and M.S. and Ph.D. degrees in electrical engineering from Stanford University.

George E.
PAKE

George E. Pake was a pioneer in the areas of physics and industrial research at Xerox Corporation. He was a Professor of Physics at both Harvard University and Stanford University, and served as Provost and Executive Vice Chancellor of Washington University. He received the National Medal of Science, and Xerox Corporation has endowed the George E. Pake Prize in recognition of Pake's outstanding achievements as a research physicist and a director of industrial research. He received B.S. and M.S. degrees in physics from Carnegie-Mellon University, and a Ph.D. degree in physics from Harvard University in 1948.

Robert B.
PALMER

Robert B. Palmer is Chairman, President, and CEO of Digital
Equipment Corporation, having held several other senior
management positions since his arrival in 1985. Prior to
Digital, he was Executive Vice President of Semiconductor
Operations at United Technologies Corporation. He joined
United Technologies in 1980, when it acquired Mostek
Corporation, a company Palmer co-founded in 1969 with a
group of fellow engineers from Texas Instruments. He is a past
member of the Boards of Directors of Sematech; the
Semiconductor Industry Association; the Semiconductor
Research Center; the Microelectronics and Computer
Technology Corporation in Austin, Texas; and several other
firms. He is currently Chairman of the Computer Systems
Policy Project, a member of the Board of Directors of Allied
Signal Inc., a member of the Board of Trustees of the Cooper
Institute for Aerobic Research and a member of the Board of
Trustees of the Committee for Economic Development (CED).
He received a B.S. degree in mathematics with high honors and
an M.S. degree in physics from Texas Tech University.

"The real revolution taking place today is the emergence of . . . location-independent computing – the ability to **access the information and services you need at anytime, from anywhere, using any device."**

Suhas
PATIL

Suhas Patil is Chairman of Cirrus Logic, which he founded in 1984. Patil received a Ph.D. degree in electrical engineering from MIT in 1970. For the next five years, he taught at MIT and served as Assistant Director of Project MAC. After that, he went to the University of Utah, where he started the VLSI (Very Large Scale Integration) group.

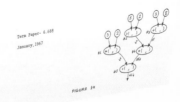

PARALLEL EVALUATION OF λ-EXPRESSION

Suhas S. Patil

Suhas Patil's original paper on "Parallel Evaluation of Lambda-Expressions," 1967.

Term Paper- 6.688

January, 1967

FIGURE 1a

Steven
PERLMAN

Steven Perlman is Co-Founder, CEO, and President of WebTV Networks, Inc., which provides internet access directly through television sets. WebTV is now part of Microsoft. Prior to that, he worked at Apple Computer, developing much of the multimedia and video technology used in the Apple Macintosh computer. In 1990, he became Managing Director of Advanced Products for General Magic, Inc. Next, he formed Catapult Entertainment, Inc., where he served as Chief Technology Officer and developed the XBand video game modem for the Sega Genesis and Super Nintendo Entertainment System. He holds eleven patents in the areas of graphics, video, animation, modems, communications, and telephony.

Lewis E.
PLATT

Lewis E. (Lew) Platt is Chairman, President, and CEO of Hewlett-Packard Company in Palo Alto, California. Platt joined HP in 1966 and has held a variety of management posts, including Executive Vice President and head of the Computer Systems Organization. He succeeded David Packard as Chairman when he retired in 1993. Platt holds a B.S. degree in mechanical engineering from Cornell University and an M.B.A. degree from the Wharton School of Business, University of Pennsylvania. In 1995, he was appointed to the Advisory Committee on Trade Policy Negotiations (ACTPN) by President Clinton and is Chairman of one of its three task forces, the World Trade Organization Task Force.

John W.
PODUSKA, SR.

John W. (Bill) Poduska, Sr., is Chairman of the Board
of Advanced Visual Systems, Inc. Prior to AVS, He was
Chairman, CEO, and a founder of Stardent. Before that,
he was founder, Chairman, CEO, and President of Apollo
Computer, Inc. Prior to Apollo, he was Vice President,
Research and Development, and a founder of Prime
Computer. He received a Ph.D. degree from MIT, where
he worked on Multics.

Kim
POLESE

Kim Polese is President and CEO of Marimba, Inc., which develops network-managed applications and multimedia programs. In early 1996, she co-founded Marimba with former Sun Microsystems, Inc., engineers Arthur van Hoff, Jonathan Payne, and Sami Shaio. Prior to Marimba, she spent more than seven years at Sun Microsystems, most recently as the Product Manager for Java. She was responsible for the Internet strategy for Java and for promoting the Java brand. Prior to joining Sun, she worked as an Applications Engineer for IntelliCorp, Inc. She holds a B.S. degree in biophysics from the University of California, Berkeley, and studied computer science at the University of Washington, Seattle.

Heidi
ROIZEN

Heidi Roizen has served as Vice President of World Wide
Developer Relations for Apple Computer and co-founder and
CEO of T/Maker Company, one of the first developers of software for the Apple Macintosh computer. She was a member of
the board of directors of the Software Publishers Association
from 1987 to 1994, and served as its President from 1988 to
1990. She was named one of the top 100 women in computing
in 1995 by McGraw Hill. She was a member of the board of
directors of the Software Publishers Association (SPA) from
1987 to 1994, and was its president from 1988 to 1990. She has
been recognized as one of the 100 most influential people in the
microcomputer industry by *MicroTimes*, *Personal Computing
Magazine*, and *Upside Magazine*. She holds a B.A. degree in
English and an M.B.A. degree from Stanford University.

Harry J.
SAAL

Harry J. Saal is Chairman of Network General Corporation and the former CEO and President of Smart Valley, Inc. He received a Ph.D. degree, magna cum laude, in high energy physics in 1969. He was then Deputy Director of the Stanford Linear Accelerator Center's Computation Group and later Visiting Associate Professor of Computer Science at the State University of New York at Buffalo. From 1973 to 1978, he worked for IBM, at the IBM Scientific Center in Haifa, Israel and the IBM General Products Division in San Jose, California. In October 1978, he founded Nestar Systems, Inc., a pioneer in local-area network systems for PCs. He has won many awards, including Ernst & Young's "Bay Area 1990 Software Entrepreneur of the Year" award. In 1995, he received the John W. Gardner Leadership Award from the American Leadership Forum. He is a well-known philanthropist in the Silicon Valley area. His personal interests include race car driving, hiking and rock climbing, genealogy, and ham radio.

Pamela
SAMUELSON

Pamela Samuelson is a specialist in computer and cyberspace law. Her work has enabled smaller software companies to compete against larger companies and has affected legal attitudes toward software protection. She was named the first faculty member at the University of California, Berkeley, School of Information Management Systems, where she teaches. Prior to that, she spent fifteen years teaching at the University of Pittsburgh law school. She is a recipient of a MacArthur Foundation "Genius" grant, among other honors. She received a B.A. degree in history and an M.S. degree in political science from the University of Hawaii, as well as a J.D. degree from Yale University. She is a compulsive reader, and once wrote part of a (still unfinished) murder mystery.

Jerry
SANDERS

W. J. (Jerry) Sanders III is the Founder and CEO of Advanced
Micro Devices. Prior to that, he was Director of Worldwide
Marketing at Fairchild Semiconductor. In May 1969, Sanders
and seven other Fairchild Semiconductor employees left to
form Advanced Micro Devices, investing a total of $50,000 to
start the company. That same year an *Innovation* magazine arti-
cle said that AMD faced "the most uncertainty." It took the
group over a year to raise $1.5 million in venture capital.
AMD's first revenue came in 1970 from a 4-bit shift register
and, in 1972, the company went public. He received his B.S.
degree in electrical engineering from the University of Illinois.

F. Grant
SAVIERS

F. Grant Saviers is President and CEO of Adaptec, Inc. Before joining Adaptec, Saviers spent twenty-five years with Digital Equipment Corporation, where he held several senior management positions, including managing a successful disk drive business. He received B.S. and M.S. degrees in engineering from Case Institute of Technology. He is a Trustee of The Computer Museum and a member of the Advisory Board of the College of Engineering of the University of California, Berkeley.

Eric
SCHMIDT

Eric Schmidt is Chairman and CEO of Novell, Inc., a
provider of networking software. Prior to joining Novell in
1997, Schmidt spent fourteen years with Sun Microsystems,
Inc., where, among other titles, he was Chief Technology
Officer. He was instrumental in the widespread acceptance of
Java, Sun's programming language, and was also responsible
for coordinating Sun's core technologies, including SPARC
microprocessors and the Solaris operating system. Prior to
joining Sun, Schmidt was a member of the research staff at
the Computer Science Lab at the Xerox Palo Alto Research
Center (PARC), and held positions at Bell Telephone Laboratories and Zilog. Schmidt holds a B.S. degree in electrical
engineering from Princeton University and a Ph.D. degree in
computer science from the University of California, Berkeley.

Paul
SEVERINO

Paul Severino is a founder and member of the board of Bay
Networks, Inc. Prior to that, in 1986, he co-founded Wellfleet
Communications, Inc., based in Billerica, Massachusetts,
where he was President and CEO until October 1994.
Wellfleet was named "The Fastest-Growing Company" in the
United States by *Fortune* magazine for both 1992 and 1993.
In 1994, Bay Networks was formed by the merger of Wellfleet
Communications and Synoptics Communications, Inc., of
Santa Clara, California. He was Chairman of the Board of
Bay Networks from 1994 until 1996. He is on the Board of
The Computer Museum.

Ray
STATA

Ray Stata is Chairman and CEO of Analog Devices. Prior to forming Analog Devices, he was a founder of Solid State Instruments and Vice President of Marketing for Kollmorgen Corporation's Inland Controls Division. He was a founder and the first President of the Massachusetts High Technology Council, and is currently a member of their Executive Committee. He holds B.S.E.E. and M.S.E.E. degrees from MIT, and serves on that institution's visiting committee of the Department of Electrical Engineering and Computer Science. He is also on the Advisory Board of the Center for Technology, Policy, and Industrial Development and the Organization Learning Center. He holds honorary degrees from Northeastern University and other institutions.

Dorothy
TERRELL

Dorothy Terrell is the former President of SunExpress, Sun Microsystems' aftermarketing company. Prior to that, she headed Digital Equipment Corporation's Application-Specific Interconnect and Packaging Group, which manufactures multichip modules. In 1995, she was named one of the "25 Black Women Who Have Made a Difference in Business" by *Black Enterprise*. She was also named one of the "Top 50 Women Line Managers in America" by *Executive Female* magazine and a "Top Ten Business Marketer" by *Business Marketer* magazine. She received a B.A. degree in history from Florida A&M University.

James
TREYBIG

James Treybig is the Founder and former President of Tandem
Computers, Inc. Prior to Tandem, he worked at Texas Instruments and Hewlett-Packard, later joining the venture capital
firm Kleiner Perkins Caufield & Byers. He received B.A. and
B.S. degrees in electrical engineering from Rice University,
and an M.B.A degree from Stanford University. He has had
a lifelong interest in ham radio.

Ralph
UNGERMANN

Ralph Ungermann is Founder, President, and CEO of First Virtual Corporation (FVC), which develops and markets multimedia networking products. Prior to this, he was co-founder and CEO of Ungermann-Bass, Inc., now called UB Networks, the first independent local-area network company in the industry. Before that he was co-founder and COO of Zilog. He received a B.S. degree in communications from the University of California, Berkeley, and an M.S. degree in computer architecture from the University of California, Irvine.

Steven C. WALSKE

Steven C. Walske is Chairman and CEO of Parametric Technology Corporation, a CAD/CAM/CAE supplier. Prior to that he was President and CEO of Multiplications Software, Inc., and was involved in that company's merger with Computer Corporation of America. He received an M.A. degree in mathematical economics from Princeton University and an M.B.A. degree from Harvard University.

Charles B.
WANG

Charles B. Wang is Chairman and CEO of Computer
Associates International, which develops mission-critical
software for business, and which is on the *Fortune* magazine
list of "Top 100 Most Valued Companies in America." He
wrote *Techno-Vision: The Executive's Survival Guide to Understanding and Managing Information Technology*. He came to
the United States in 1952 from Shanghai, China, where
he was born. He received a B.S. degree in mathematics from
Queens College. He is an avid cook and basketball player.

John
WARNOCK

entrepreneurs

John Warnock has been a pioneer in the desktop publishing field since the 1970s, when he worked as Principal Scientist at the Xerox Palo Alto Research Center (PARC). He founded Adobe Systems in 1982 with Charles M. Geschke, and is currently Chairman and CEO. He is also on the boards of Netscape Communications, Red Brick Systems, and Evans & Sutherland. He has received many awards, including the ACM SIGGRAPH Computer Achievement Award and the 1991 Ernst & Young's "Entrepreneur of the Year" award. He holds a B.S. degree in mathematics and philosophy, an M.S. degree in mathematics, and a Ph.D. degree in electrical engineering, all from the University of Utah.

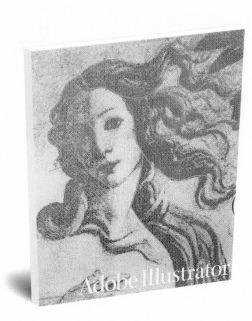

Adobe Illustrator, a pioneering desktop publishing program.

Phillip E. WHITE

Phillip E. White is the former President, Chairman, and CEO of Informix Software. Before that he was President of Wyse Technology, Inc., and Vice President of Sales and Marketing at Altos Computer Systems. He also spent fifteen years at IBM in sales and marketing. He has received many awards, including the Legend in Leadership Award from the Leadership & Career Studies' Goizueta Business School at Emory University. *Financial World* magazine honored him as "CEO of the Year" for the third consecutive year in 1995. He received a B.A. degree in business from Illinois Wesleyan University and an M.B.A. degree from the University of Illinois, Urbana.

John
YOUNG

John Young retired in 1992 as CEO of Hewlett-Packard Company. In 1994, he was named Co-Chairman of the President's Committee of Advisors on Science and Technology. He is Founding Chairman of the Computer Systems Policy Project, an affiliation of American computer company chief executive officers who formulate and advocate public-policy recommendations on issues that are of critical importance to the computer industry. He is also a member of the Council on Competitiveness, a private-sector group chartered to improve the competitiveness of U.S. business. He is a Director of Wells Fargo & Co., Chevron, Novell, SmithKline Beecham, Shaman Pharmaceuticals, Affymetrix, Abiotic Systems, and General Magic, and is a member of The Business Council. He is currently pursuing interests in the National Information Infrastructure as the Chairman of Smart Valley, Inc.

entrepreneurs

334

Communicators

336

Fortunately, the computer industry does listen to its talkers. And the industry loves to talk about itself, both to itself and to others. It does so online, offline, at conferences, and in computer magazine columns. Journalists, politicians, technocrats, public relations specialists, and sages fan the flames of discourse. They critique, sell, set policy, interpret, praise, complain, and gossip. They anticipate trends, act as watchdogs, testify before Congress, and take stands. They are the conscience of an industry that grew up collectively in the 1970s, when the microprocessor burst on the scene and the PC followed close behind. Because of this common period of "adolescence," the computer industry has retained a strong sense of collegiality. Remarkably, nearly everyone knows everyone else, or knows someone who does. One to two "degrees of separation" still suffice in an industry grown big enough to move the stock market up or down on a given day.

Stewart
ALSOP

Stewart Alsop is a highly visible personality in the computing industry. He is a columnist for *Fortune* magazine and the Executive Producer of *Agenda*, an annual conference attended by senior executives of software companies. Before that he was Editor-in-Chief of *InfoWorld*, Executive Vice President of InfoWorld Publishing Company, Executive Editor of *Inc*, and founder of *P.C. Letter*, an industry newsletter he wrote for eight years. He is currently a partner in New Enterprise Associates, a high-tech venture capital firm. He and his older brother Joseph are the sons of the late political journalist Stewart Alsop and the nephews of Joseph Alsop, the Washington-based national columnist.

Gwen BELL

Gwen Bell is the Founding President and Board Member of The Computer Museum in Boston, Massachusetts, and Director of Collections for The Computer Museum History Center, Silicon Valley, California. In 1979, she founded The Computer Museum based on the model of the Corning Glass Museum. In 1981, she sensed the clear need for a non-profit, independent Computer Museum and assembled an international Board of Directors, which included Robert Noyce, Patrick McGovern, Koji Kobayashi, and Kenneth H. Olsen (Chairman). Bell served as President of the ACM from 1992 to 1994, for which she is the current Chair of the awards and the nominating committees. Prior to that, she was a United Nations Consultant and an Associate Professor of Urban Affairs at the Graduate School of Public and International Affairs at the University of Pittsburgh. She received a Ph.D. degree in geography from Clark University and an M.C.R.P. degree from the Graduate School of Design, Harvard University, as well as honorary degrees from Simmons College and Clark University.

George
COLONY

George Colony is Founder and President of Forrester Research, Inc., where he analyzes technology. He started the company with the belief that the PC would have a major impact on business, and is particularly interested in client/server issues and the phenomenon of the "New Customer Connection." He is a frequent speaker at industry symposia in the United States, Europe, and the Far East. He is a graduate of Harvard University.

Andy
CUNNINGHAM

Andy Cunningham began her career in public relations
working at Regis McKenna, Inc., as a Group Account Manager
on the Apple Computer account, and led the team that
introduced the Macintosh computer in 1984. She is currently
the President and Founder of Cunningham Communication,
which counts Motorola, Inc., among its many clients. She is
also Founder and Chairperson of the Interactive Media
Festival, an international event that links interactive technologies with the media arts. She is on the boards of The Computer
Museum, Construct, Inc., the Djerassi Foundation, First Floor,
Inc., and the Nueva School. She is an officer in the Young
Presidents' organization. Prior to her current position, she was
at the Burson-Marsteller agency in Chicago, Illinois. She
received a B.A. degree in English from Northwestern
University.

Esther
DYSON

Esther Dyson is President and Owner of EDventure Holdings, a company that focuses on emerging technologies worldwide, with a particular emphasis on Eastern Europe and the former Soviet Republics. EDventure publishes *Release 1.0*, an industry newsletter, and sponsors two annual conferences, the PC Forum, an industry staple for over twenty years, and the EDventures Hi Tech Forum. Dyson is Chairman of the Electronic Frontier Foundation and was a member of the U.S. National Information Infrastructure Advisory Council. She speaks fluent Russian and swims for at least one hour every day.

"'Owning' intellectual property is like owning land: You need to keep investing in it to get a payoff; you can't simply sit back and collect rent."

Gideon I.
GARTNER

Gideon I. Gartner founded Gartner Group, Inc., in 1979, was President, CEO, and Chairman until 1991, and was Chairman until 1992. The company provides decision support in the computer, telecommunications, and office industries. It went public in 1986 and was ranked among the best small companies in America by *Business Week*, being number one in profitability in 1987. In 1990, he led a leveraged buyout of the firm, and in 1993 sold his equity position and severed his ties. He is currently Chairman of the Board and CEO of Giga Information Group, an acquisition-based start-up in the information technology field. Prior to this, he founded Soundview Financial Group and was a partner at Oppenheimer & Company. He received a B.S. degree in mechanical engineering from MIT and an M.B.A. degree from the Sloan School. He is a Sustaining Fellow Life Member of MIT and is on the board of the Society for Information Management, where he is Special Appointee to the President.

Anita JONES

While a faculty member at Carnegie-Mellon University, Anita Jones contributed to the development of software systems for parallel computation in the context of the Cm* and C.mmp projects. She is a co-founder of Tartan Laboratories. In addition to working in the university and in private industry, Jones served in the U.S. government as the Director of Defense Research and Engineering during President Clinton's first term, where she oversaw the Defense Department's science and technology program. She earned a B.A. degree in mathematics from Rice University, an M.A. degree in English literature from the University of Texas at Austin, and a Ph.D. degree in computer science from Carnegie-Mellon University.

"**Investment in research is the water and fertilizer** necessary to bring forth the flowers of the future."

Brenda
LAUREL

Brenda Laurel is a computer games pioneer with a deep interest in the primal power of storytelling. She specializes in human-computer interface design, virtual reality, and interactive fiction. She has worked at Atari, Apple Computer, LucasArts Entertainment, and Paramount New Media, and is currently Vice President/Design of Purple Moon, an entertainment company whose products are designed for girls. Purple Moon grew out of research she did at Interval Research Corporation. She began her career as a computer game designer and programmer at CyberVision, Inc. She co-founded Telepresence Research, Inc., and has served as a consultant to Apple Computer, Citibank, Fujitsu Laboratories, Lucasfilm Games, Sony Pictures, and Paramount New Media. She earned M.F.A. and Ph.D. degrees in theatre from Ohio State University and a B.A. degree from DePauw University. She lives with her partner, their three daughters, and three cats in the Santa Cruz mountains of Northern California.

Edward
MARKEY

Edward Markey, U.S. Representative from Massachusetts, chaired the House Telecommunications Subcommittee in the U.S. Congress for eight years and continues to serve as its highest-ranking Democrat. He is the author of major laws opening up the cable industry to competition from satellites, requiring the broadcast industry to serve the educational needs of children, launching the wireless revolution, and providing for the transition to advanced digital television. He has successfully fought to break down historic monopolies, promote public-interest obligations, and ensure universal access to online information, especially in K-12 schools and classrooms – a key policy of the Telecommunications Bill of 1996.

He also coined the term *V-Chip* and successfully amended the telecommunications bill on the House floor to include this blocking technology in all new television sets. He is also interested in ensuring privacy and security on the emerging "information superhighways." He earned a B.A. degree from Boston College and a J.D. degree from Boston College Law School.

"The information age poses no greater test than finding ways to spread technology across income groups and into our poorest schools. **We must teach all Americans to use the tools of the digital era or suffer the consequences.** It is a test we cannot afford to fail."

John
MARKOFF

John Markoff is West Coast Correspondent for *The New York Times*, where he covers Silicon Valley, computers, and information technologies. Prior to his work at the *Times,* he covered Silicon Valley for the *San Francisco Examiner.* He was also a reporter for *InfoWorld* and the West Coast Technical Editor for *BYTE.* With Katie Hafner he co-authored *Cyberpunk: Outlaws and Hackers on the Computer Frontier* (1991*).* He and Lenny Siegel also co-authored *The High Cost of High Tech* (1985). In 1996, *Takedown: The Pursuit and Capture of America's Most Wanted Computer Outlaw* appeared, co-authored by Markoff and Tsutomu Shimomura.

Patrick McGOVERN

Patrick McGovern is Founder and Chairman of International Data Group (IDG) in Boston, Massachusetts, a computer publishing, research, and exposition-management company, which began in 1964 and now has annual revenues of over $1.4 billion. His publishing career began as a student at MIT when he became Associate Editor of *Computers and Automation*, the first U.S. computer magazine. He launched *ComputerWorld* in 1967, a weekly magazine that covers industry and product news. Since 1964, he has launched over 275 computer magazines and newspapers in 75 countries, including *InfoWorld, MacWorld, Network World,* and *PC World.* The ... *For Dummies* book series is published by IDG and has sold more than 30 million copies. *ComputerWorld* even has a "North Pole" online edition. Earnest & Young named him "Entrepreneur of the Year," one of many awards he has won.

"My father told me, 'Son, there are only six words that express what you do in business: **find a need and fill it.**'"

Regis
McKENNA

Regis McKenna rose to fame in the early days of the personal computing industry by shepherding the public image and marketing of such companies as Apple Computer, Inc., and Intel Corporation. He is currently Chairman of the McKenna Group, a management and marketing consulting firm. He has worked with many entrepreneurial start-ups over the years, including America Online (AOL), Businessland, Compaq Computer Corporation, Electronic Arts, Genentech, Lotus Development, Microsoft, and many others. In 1985, he wrote the first book devoted to the marketing of high-technology companies, *The Regis Touch*. His other titles include *Whose Afraid of Big Blue?* (1989) and *Real Time: Preparing for the Never Satisfied Customer* (1997). He is also a Venture Partner with Kleiner Perkins Caufield & Byers. He has received honorary Ph.D. degrees from Duquesne University and Saint Vincent College.

"We are more part of the electronics industry than the PR industry.

I've never studied public relations; I've studied technology."

Nicholas P.
NEGROPONTE

Nicholas P. Negroponte is Director and Founder of the Media Laboratory and Jerome B. Wiesner Professor of Media Technology at MIT. He is also the author of the best-selling book *Being Digital* (1995). He serves as a consultant to both government and industry on the human-computer interface and on new technologies for information, education, and publishing. He founded the Architecture Machine Group at MIT, responsible for many new approaches to the human-computer interface. In 1980, he served a term as Founding Chairman of the International Federation of Information Processing Societies' Computers in Everyday Life Program in Amsterdam. Two years later, he became the first Executive Director of the Paris-based World Center for Personal Computation and Human Development. Recently, he has served on the science advisory boards of Computervision, Mead Imaging, and the U.S. Department of Health and Human Services' Technology and the Handicapped Program. He received B.A. and M.A. degrees in architecture from MIT.

Naomi O.
SELIGMAN

Naomi O. Seligman is a Senior Partner of the Research
Board, which she co-founded in 1969. The Board investigates
computing and communications issues and trends for a group
of senior information systems executives from 65 large
international corporations. The confidential research exam-
ines the best ways to organize information systems
organizations, how to improve productivity, the implications
of shifting demographics on the work force, the Japanese
computer industry, and so on. To maintain objectivity, the
Board does not allow vendors to participate. Before forming
the Research Board, she was a Vice President of the Diebold
Group. She is a Director of The Computer Museum and
holds memberships in many professional societies. She
received a B.A. degree from Vassar College and a graduate
degree from the London School of Economics.

Richard
SHAFFER

Richard (Dick) Shaffer is the Principal of Technologic Partners, which he founded in 1984. He also edits and publishes the company's publications, which include *ComputerLetter* and *VentureFinance*. Technologic reports on strategic business and financial issues in technology and analyzes and predicts trends. Shaffer also speaks frequently to industry and investment groups, and contributes a regular column to *Forbes*. He was also Science and Technology Editor of the *Wall Street Journal*. He received a B.A. degree in philosophy from the University of Oklahoma.

Richard
TENNANT

Richard Tennant is a syndicated cartoonist who *Forbes* calls "the father of the computer cartoon." He has been the weekly editorial cartoonist for *ComputerWorld* and *Federal Computer Week* since 1988. He draws "The 5th Wave" cartoon series, which appears regularly in *PC Magazine*, *ComputerWorld*, *Federal Computer Week*, *FamilyPC*, and assorted corporate publications. He also draws the cartoons for the popular *. . . For Dummies* book series. Two collections of his cartoons have appeared in book form, and he has added comic relief to many technical documents and marketing brochures.

Sherry
TURKLE

Sherry Turkle is Professor of the Sociology of Science at MIT and author of *Life on the Screen: Identity in the Age of the Internet* (1995). She specializes in the study of people's relationships with technology, particularly with computers. Her most recent research focuses on the psychology and sociology of computer-mediated communication. She has been featured on the covers of *Wired* and *Technology Review* and was named "Woman of the Year" by *Ms*, as well as a member of "America's New Leadership Class" by *Esquire*. She has spoken about the impact of the computer on many radio and television shows, and has pursued her research with support from the National Science Foundation, the MacArthur Foundation, the Guggenheim Foundation, and the Rockefeller Foundation. She received a joint Ph.D. degree in personality psychology and sociology from Harvard University. She is a licensed clinical psychologist and a graduate and affiliate member of the Boston Psychoanalytic Institute.

Lawrence
WEBER

Lawrence (Larry) Weber is Chairman and CEO of Weber
Public Relations Worldwide of Cambridge, Massachusetts, the
tenth largest public relations agency in the world, as well as
Chairman of The Weber Group. He has worked with many
high-tech clients, including Lotus Development Corporation,
America Online (AOL), 3Com, and Bell Atlantic, as well as
non-high-tech companies such as WalMart and Marshalls. He
is also Chairman of the Board of Trustees of The Computer
Museum and Chairman of the Board of the Massachusetts
Interactive Media Council (MIMC). He received a B.A. degree
from Denison University in Ohio and a master's degree from
Antioch College in Oxford, England.

William A.
WULF

William A. Wulf is the President of the National Academy of Engineering. He is on leave from the University of Virginia, where he is a University Professor and the AT&T Professor of Engineering and Applied Science. At the university he has done research on computer architecture and computer security, and has worked to help humanities scholars exploit information technology. Prior to that, he served as Associate Director of the National Science Foundation, where he was deeply involved in developing the High Performance Computing and Communication Initiative. He is a Fellow of the ACM, the IEEE, and the AAAS. He received a B.S. degree in engineering physics and an M.S. degree in electrical engineering from the University of Illinois, and a Ph.D. degree in computer science from the University of Virginia.

Venture Capitalists

"Investing in high technology was a calling, and monetary reward was the by-product of a successful mission. The higher goal was to create something enduring, a growing enterprise that delivers products, employees people, and enhances the wealth of its stockholders."

- JERRY KAPLAN, COMMENTING ON JOHN DOERR (OF KLIENER PERKINS CAUFIELD AND BYERS) IN *STARTUP!*

376

As Harold McGraw once said about the publishing world, "My assets get up and go home everyday at 5 PM." Venture capitalists are as interested in the management of a company as they are in its products and services. They have to be – they are, after all, trying to create the maximum wealth in the minimum time. Jerry Kaplan's quote about venture capitalist John Doerr exemplifies the highest calling of the venture capitalist – a specialist who does much more than lend money, and whose role is often misunderstood. Venture capitalists and bankers work in the rarefied and leveraged world of high tech finance, hoping to obtain a return of, perhaps, three to five times their initial investment in just a few years. They become part of the company, sitting on boards, and keeping an extremely close eye on management. They become working partners in the business, often consolidating two or more businesses in the process. The bedrock companies upon which the PC industry was built could not have achieved their success as quickly as they did without the seminal influence of the venture capitalists and bankers.

377

William H. DAVIDOW

William H. Davidow is a General Partner of Mohr, Davidow Ventures, in Menlo Park, California, a venture capital firm specializing in high-tech investments. Before that he held a number of positions at Intel Corporation, including Senior Vice President of Marketing and Sales and Vice President of the Microcomputer Systems Division. He wrote *Marketing High Technology* (1986), *Total Customer Service* (1989), and *The Virtual Corporation* (1992). He is also Chairman of Rambus, Inc., and FormFactor, Inc., and a Director of Chromatic Research, Inc., and Vantive Corporation. He received B.S. and M.S. degrees in electrical engineering from Dartmouth College, and a Ph.D. degree in electrical engineering from Stanford University. He holds several patents.

"**Marketing is civilized warfare. . .** Your competitor's job is to

capture business and then defend that new parameter. So is yours."

John
DOERR

John Doerr joined Intel Corporation in 1974, just as they introduced the 8080 microprocessor. He remained at Intel in various engineering and marketing positions, and in 1980 joined Kleiner Perkins Caufield & Byers, where he sponsored a series of investments, including Compaq, Cypress, Intuit, Macromedia, Netscape, Lotus, Millennium, S3, Sun Microsystems, and Symantec. Since the mid-1970s, he and his partners have invested over $1.3 billion in 250 U.S. technology ventures. Doerr was the founding CEO of Silicon Compilers, and currently serves on the boards of Intuit, Macromedia, Netscape, and Sun Microsystems. His recent interests include education, the Internet, and biotechnology genomics. He received B.S. and M.S. degrees in electrical engineering from Rice University, and an M.B.A. degree from the Harvard Graduate School of Business Administration.

William R. HAMBRECHT

William R. Hambrecht is a founder and Chairman of
Hambrecht & Quist LLC, an investment banking firm
specializing in emerging growth companies. He co-founded the
company with the late George Quist in 1968. Their goal was
to develop a regional investment bank that could serve small,
rapidly growing companies in Silicon Valley. Hambrecht
managed over $550 million in venture capital investments
in such companies as Evans & Sutherland, Convergent
Technologies, Genentech, People Express Airlines, Apollo
Computer, and VLSI Technology. More recent companies
include Adobe Systems, Advanced Fiber Communications,
Inc., MIPS Computer Systems, Read-Rite, Red Brick, Sybase,
Syntellect, and Xilinx. Prior to co-founding Hambrecht &
Quist, he was a Vice President and Manager of the West Coast
Corporate Finance Department of Francis I. DuPont &
Company. He is a cum laude graduate of Princeton University.
He cultivates grapes at his vineyard in Sonoma Valley,
California, and is Chairman of Belvedere Winery.

Franklin Pitcher
JOHNSON

Franklin Pitcher (Pitch) Johnson founded Asset Management Company of Palo Alto, California, in 1965, which has since invested in over 100 companies, including Applied Bio Systems, Conductus, Hybritech, Octel, Qume, Red Brick Systems, Remedy, Sierra Semiconductor, Teradyne, and Verity. Johnson also helped form European Renaissance Capital, a venture capital company concentrating on Eastern Europe and the former Soviet Republics. He is Chairman of Boole and Babbage and a director of Amgen, ICED Pharmaceuticals, and Tandem Computers. He received a B.S. degree in mechanical engineering from Stanford University and an M.B.A. degree from Harvard University.

Vinod
KHOSLA

At the age of 27, Vinod Khosla was a co-founder and the first CEO of Sun Microsystems, Inc., whose main venture capital came from Kleiner Perkins Caufield & Byers, a high-technology venture capital firm for which he is now a General Partner. Ward Winslow has noted that Khosla had a "burning desire" to become a millionaire by the age of thirty. Khosla also co-founded Daisy Systems. He serves on the boards of Concentric Network, Excite, Inc., Fiberlane Communications, Juniper Networks, OnLive! Technologies, PictureTel, Spectrum Holobyte, the 3DO Company, and Total Entertainment Network. He received a bachelor of technology degree from the Indian Institute of Technology in New Delhi, an M.S. degree in biomedical engineering from Carnegie-Mellon University, and an M.B.A. degree from Stanford University.

Floyd
KVAMME

Since 1984, Floyd Kvamme has been a Partner at Kleiner Perkins Caufield & Byers, a high-technology venture capital firm. He currently serves on the board of NeoVista Solutions, Photon Dynamics, Power Integrations, Iriquint Semiconductor, Harmonic Lightwaves, Dynachip, Prism Solutions, Brio, and Gemfire. Prior to that, he was involved in the early days at National Semiconductor and, later, Apple Computer. He received a B.S. degree in electrical engineering from the University of California, Berkeley, and an M.S. degree in electrical engineering from Syracuse University. His special hobby is raising koi in his backyard pond.

David F.
MARQUARDT

David F. Marquardt is Founding General Partner of August Capital, a private venture capital firm formed in 1995 in Menlo Park, California. He was a Founding Partner of Technology Venture Investors in 1980, and has since served on the boards of Microsoft, Sun Microsystems, Adaptec, Seagate Technology, Archive, Auspex Systems, Visioneer, and others. He has privately invested in Chronicle Publishing, Farallon Computing, Grand Junction Networks, QuickLogic, and Synaptics. He was twice voted "Venture Capitalist of the Year" by *Dataquest/Venture* and *Upside*. He received a B.S. degree in mechanical engineering from Columbia University and an M.B.A. degree from Stanford University.

Sandford R.
ROBERTSON

Sanford R. (Sandy) Robertson co-founded Robertson, Stephens & Company, a San Francisco-based investment banking firm, in 1978. The company has invested in Cypress Semiconductor, Sun Microsystems, Seagate, AOL, Lotus, and Ascend, among many others. By 1997, the firm had financed 621 companies in 26 states and ten foreign countries, raising $34.7 billion in the process. In 1972, Robertson introduced Eugene Kleiner to Thomas Perkins, who later became founders of Kleiner Perkins Caufield & Byers. He received B.B.A. and M.B.A. degrees from the University of Michigan.

"Financing emerging growth companies is very satisfying.

You raise the money and the next year the building is up and the parking lot

is full of new employees' cars. It must have the same satisfactions as being an architect

and seeing the tangible results of your work."

Arthur
ROCK

Arthur Rock made his first dollar as a child selling candy in his father's store. Since then, he has become one of the best-known venture capitalists in Silicon Valley. He was an original investor in Apple Computer, Intel, Diasonics, Scientific Data Systems, and Fairchild Semiconductor, among others. He was a General Partner of Davis and Rock in the 1960s, and founded Arthur Rock and Associates in 1969. He has served as a Director on the boards of Xerox Corporation, Teledyne, Inc., Apple Computer, Intel Corp., and Echelon. He formulated "Rock's Law," which he calls "a very small addendum" to Moore's Law: The cost of capital equipment to build semiconductors will double every four years. He received a B.S. degree from Syracuse University and an M.B.A. degree from Harvard University.

"Nearly every mistake I've made has been because I picked the wrong people, not the wrong idea."

Benjamin M.
ROSEN

Benjamin M. (Ben) Rosen is Chairman of the Board of
Compaq Computer Corporation. He is also Chairman of
Sevin Rosen Funds, a venture capital firm that has invested in
over eighty computer, software, telecommunications, health-
care, electronics, and other technology start-up companies.
Among the Sevin Rosen companies that have gone public are
Compaq, Lotus, Silicon Graphics, Electronic Arts, and
Quarterdeck Office Systems. In 1992, he was named the
"Number One Executive in the Personal Computer Industry"
by *Computer Reseller News* and one of the "Ten Legends of
the PC Industry" by *CRN*. He is also Chairman of Rosen
Motors Corporation, which develops turbo-flywheel hybrid-
electric power trains. He received a B.S. degree in electrical
engineering from Stanford University and an M.B.A. degree
from Columbia Business School.

John
SHOCH

John Shoch received a B.A. degree in political science, and M.S. and Ph.D. degrees in computer science, all from Stanford University. In 1971, he joined the Xerox Palo Alto Research Center (PARC), where he worked on the Smalltalk system, the Ethernet networking protocol, packet radio, and "worm" programs. He later served as Executive Assistant to the Chairman of Xerox and as President of the Office Systems Division. Since 1985, he has been a General Partner at Asset Management in Palo Alto, specializing in venture capital investments in the computer industry. He is a Director of Remedy, Red Brick Systems, and Conductus.

Donald T.
VALENTINE

Donald T. Valentine founded Sequoia Capital in 1972, which has financed over 400 technology companies in the areas of semiconductors, personal computer software, digital entertainment, and internetworking, most notably Cisco Systems, LSI Logic, and Microchip Technology. In the early days of personal computing, he was a Director of Atari, Apple, and Electronic Arts, and has served on the boards of Oracle, Altos, and Pyramid. He is currently Chairman of Network Appliance. Before Sequoia, Valentine co-founded National Semiconductor. He is Chairman of the Stanford University Venture Fund and continues his quest to play every championship golf course in the world.

Ann
WINBLAD

Ann Winblad is a co-founding Partner of Hummer Winblad Venture Partners, a venture capital firm founded in 1989 that focuses exclusively on software investing. Winblad has over twenty years of experience in the software industry, beginning her career as a programmer. In 1976, she co-founded Open Systems, Inc., an accounting software supplier for personal and networked computers. She initially invested $500 in the company and ultimately sold it for $15.1 million in 1983. She has been a strategic planning consultant for systems and application software firms, including IBM, Microsoft, Price Waterhouse, and numerous start-ups. She co-authored *Object-Oriented Software* (1990) and has served on the boards of several software start-ups. She received a B.A. degree in mathematics and business administration and an M.A. degree in international economics and education from the College of St. Thomas, Minneapolis.

Index

407

About the Association For Computing Machinery and The Computer Museum

Wizards and Their Wonders: Portraits In Computing is co-published by the Association for Computing Machinery (ACM) and The Computer Museum.

THE ASSOCIATION FOR COMPUTING MACHINERY

The Association for Computing Machinery (ACM) is a major force in advancing the skills of information technology professionals and students. The ACM serves its global membership by delivering cutting edge technical information and transferring ideas from theory to practice. The ACM, with its world-class journals and magazines, dynamic special interest groups, numerous conferences, workshops, and electronic forums, is a primary resource to the information technology field.

The ACM was founded in 1947, a year after the first successful electronic digital computer (ENIAC) was unveiled. It became the first and remains the largest international scientific and educational computer society in the world. Its founders and first members were mathematicians and electrical engineers, one of them being John Mauchly, the co-inventor of the ENIAC. They formed the Association as a forum for the exchange of information, knowledge and ideas that would advance the development of computing technology and its emergent industry.

Over the years, ACM's membership has included most of the men and women who led the world into what is now called the Information Age. Their activities are honored both in ACM publications and in ACM awards for distinctive contributions to the field, such as the A.M. Turing Award and the Grace Murray Hopper Award. ACM members include computer practitioners, developers, researchers, educators, engineers and managers with a significant interest in the creation and application of information technologies. For additional information about the ACM, see http://www.acm.org on the World Wide Web; telephone 1-800-342-6626.

THE COMPUTER MUSEUM

Founded in 1982, The Computer Museum in Boston is the first institution in the world devotedly solely to people and computers. The mission of the Museum is to educate and inspire people of all ages and backgrounds from around the world through dynamic exhibitions and programs on the technology, application, and impact of computers, and to preserve and celebrate the history of and promote the understanding of computers worldwide. It is also an international resource for research into the history of computing.

The Museum features more than 170 interactive exhibits that explore the history, technology, applications and impact of computing. In 1996, The Computer Museum History Center was established in Silicon Valley to further fulfill the Museum's mission as an international resource on the history of computing. The History Center is home to the largest archive of computing artifacts in the world. In addition, through the Museum's Computer Clubhouse after-school program, thousands of inner-city youths in Boston, New York, and Germany are expanding their horizons using computers to work on projects that interest them.

The Computer Museum Network (www.tcm.org) reinterprets the Museum's elements for the global audience of the Internet through Java-enabled, interactive exhibits, an historic timeline, educational materials, and a store. The Computer Museum is located at 300 Congress Street, Boston, Massachusetts 02210, (617) 426-2800. Our site is www.tcm.org.

CREDITS

PORTRAITS: All portraits in this book were photographed by Louis Fabian Bachrach III, with the following exceptions:

Howard Aiken, page 4; John Atanasoff, page 6; Seymour Cray, page 8; J. Presper Eckert, page 10; Grace Murray Hopper, page 12; John Kemeny, page 14; John Mauchly, page 16; Allen Newell, page 18 (courtesy the Carnegie Mellon University Archives); George Stibitz, page 20; John von Neumann, page 22; Thomas Watson, Jr., page 24; Thomas Watson, Sr., page 26 (photograph by Y. Karsh); Steven P. Jobs, page 108 (photograph by Robert Holmgren).

ARTIFACT PHOTOS: All artifact photos are courtesy of The Computer Museum with the following exceptions: Dan Bricklin, page 56; Douglas Engelbart, page 76; George Riley, page 78; Copyright Connection Machine Services, Inc., 1997, page 104; Pixar, page 126; Benoit Mandelbrot, page 130; Fayfoto, page 144.

SOURCES

Much of the information contained in this book came directly from resumes and short biographies furnished by the subjects. In addition, two particularly useful books were: *Computer Pioneers* by J.A.N. Lee (IEEE Computer Society Press, Los Alamitos, California, 1995) and *Portraits Of Success: Impressions of Silicon Valley Pioneers* by Carolyn Caddes (Tioga Publishing Co., Palo Alto, California, 1986). I am grateful to both authors for their pioneering research.

Additional information for the biographies and quotes came from the following sources:

Aiken, Howard	Quote from Slater, *Portraits in Silicon*, p. 88
Allen, Fran	Annals of the History of Computing, 4/4, p. 364; Wexelblat, *History of Programming Languages*, p. 57; http://www.cs.yale.edu/homes/tap/present-women-Biographical information html
Amdahl, Gene	Lee, p. 22
Andreessen, Marc	http://home3.netscape.com/comprod/exec_team.html; http://www.chem.brown.edu/chem31/andreessen.html Quote from *Time* magazine 12/5/94)
Atanasoff, John	Quote from Slater, p. 59.; Biographical information from Mollenhoff, *Atanasoff, Forgotten Father of the Computer*, p. 160
Backus, John	http://go.cis.usouthal.edu/faculty/daigle/project1/1957fort.htm; Quote in biography from Wexelblat, *History of Programming Languages* , p. 30; Caption quote from Wexelblat, p. 27
Barksdale, Jim	http://home.netscape.com/comprod/exec_team.html
Baskett, Forrest	Quote from *R & D* Magazine, Nov 1995, p. 18.
Bezos, Jeff	http://www.annonline.com/interviews/970106/biography.html; Quote from: *Publishers Weekly*, Nov 4 1996, p. 24
Blinn, Jim	http://www.research.microsoft.com/research/graphics/blinn/; Quote from graduation address at: http://www.research.microsoft.com/research/graphics/blinn/parsons.htm; http://wwww.wired.com/wired/4.07/features/microsoft3d.html
Braun, Jeff	Quote from: *Red Herring*, 12/94
Bricklin, Dan	Quote from *Programmers at Work*, Lammers, p. 138
Brooks, Fred	Quote from: http://www.phlab.missouri.edu/~ccgreg/Quotes/Illuminating/Programming_Quotes.html; Metcalfe Quote from *New York Times*, 7/15/96, p. D7
Buchanan, Bruce	http://www.cs.pitt.edu/isl/BGB/Welcome.html; see also: http://lieber.www.media.mit.edu/people/lieber/Lieberary/AI/Fifth-Gen/Fifth-Gen.html
Canion, Rod	Quote cited by Dr. Raymond Smilor, Ewing Marion Kauffman Foundation, from http://www.fed.org/Leading-Companies/nov96/lead.htm; Biographical notes from http://www.jii.com/digitalcentury/encyclo/update/Canion.html
Carlston, Doug	Biographical notes from http://www.jii.com/digitalcentury/encyclo/update/brodbund.html; Quoted in *Industry Week*, April 17 1995, p. 24
Cerf, Vint	ACM97 conference speech, 3/97
Chowning, John	http://cmn19.stanford.edu/~brent/wiredsidebar.html;; http://grasshopper.ucsd.edu/95_96/bobw/rock_bios.html

Corrigan, Wilfred J.	Biography from http://207.240.86.21/mediakit/unit3_1a.html#ExecutiveBio
Costello, Joe	Biography notes from *Electronic Business News*, at http://techweb.cmp.com/ebn/costello.html
Davidow, William H.	Quote from *Marketing High Technology: An Insider's View* by William H. Davidow; Free Press, 1986, p. 1
Dell, Michael	Quotes from *Newsbytes*, 2/1/95
Dyson, Esther	Quote from Progress & Freedom Foundation's Aspen Summit, 1995, at http://www.microtimes.com/mt100.html
Ellison, Lawrence	Biography notes from *San Francisco Business Times* 1/9/97; Quote from *Electronic Business News* at http://techweb.cmp.com/ebn/ellison.html
Engelbart, Douglas	http://gneiss.coe.berkeley.edu/~epa/Matrix/96f/engelbart.html; personal page is at: http://kk.ucsb.edu/culler/engelbart.html; see also: http://www.webhistory.org/historyday/abstracts.html#doug
Engelberger, Joseph F.	Quote cited in: http://robby.caltech.edu/~mason/Quotes.html#onrobotics; http://www.owirobot.com/history.html; see also Ralston, *Encyclopedia of Computer Science, Third Edition*, p. 1167
Estrin, Judy	http://www.precept.com/company/; Quote from: http://www.geekweek.com/estrin.html
Everett, Robert	Biography notes from: *Project Whirlwind: The History of A Pioneer Computer* by Redmond and Smith, p.15; Quote from: Redmond and Smith, op. cit., p. 241
Feigenbaum, Ed	http://www.stsc.hill.af.mil/CrossTalk/1995/mar/Feigenba.html; Quote from Caddes, p. 68; also, for biography: http://www-soe.stanford.edu/compsci/faculty/Feigenbaum_Edward.html
Ferren, Bran	http://www.acm.org/acm97/conference/ferren_flores_mann.html; http://www.epcc.ed.ac.uk/martinwe/www4/report.html
Forrester, Jay	Quote from a paper delivered to the Modern Calculator Machinery and Numerical Methods Symposium, 1948; cited in *Project Whirlwind: The History of A Pioneer Computer* by Redmond and Smith, p. 225
Frankston, Bob	Quote from Programmers at Work, Lammers, p. 158.
Galvin, Robert	Biography from: http://vm1.hqadmin.doe.gov/seab/gal_bios.html
Garlick, Larry	Quote from *Communications Week*, March 18 1996, p. 64
Grove, Andy	Grove's Law Quoted in *New York Times*, 7/15/96, p. D7.; *Fortune* magazine interview, 2/17/97; Biography from: http://www.microtest.com/cdh/intel/news/events/telecom/keynote/grove biographicalinformationhtm
Hambrecht, William	Quote from Levering, et al, The Computer Entrepreneurs, p. 424
Heilmeier, George	*EDGE, On & About AT&T* Magazine, Jan 27 1997; Quote from: America's Network Magazine, Sept 15 1996, p. 30
Hertzfeld, Andy	http://wwww.wired.com/wired/2.04/features/general.magic.html; Quote from: Mobilis online magazine, August 1995, at http://www.volksware.com/mobilis/august.95/hertz1.htm
Hopper, Grace Murray	Quote from Billings, *Grace Hopper: Navy Admiral and Computer Pioneer*, p. 51
Hopper, Max	Biography from EDGE: Work-Group Computing Report, April 3, 1995, p. 76.; Quote from *Enterprise Systems Journal*, Jan., 1995, p. 14

House, Charles	Biography from http://www.baynetworks.com/News/Press/9610301.html; Quote from *Communications of the ACM*
Jones, Anita	Biography from: http://csis.ee.virginia.edu/faculty/ajones.html
Kahn, Philippe	Quote from *InfoWorld*, 12/11/95, p. 29
Kaplan, Jerry	Quote from: *Startup*, by Jerry Kaplan, p. 294; Biography from: http://www.hmco.com/hmco/trade/low/nonfiction/catalog/AboutAuthor0-395-71133-9.html
Kapor, Mitchell	Biography notes from: http://ei.cs.vt.edu/~history/Kapor.Schneider.html; Quotes from: http://www.cd.sc.ehu.es/DOCS/nearnet.gnn.com/mag/10_93/articles/kapor/nkapor.whole.html
Kay, Alan	Quote from: http://www.phlab.missouri.edu/~ccgreg/Quotes/Illuminating/Programming_Quotes.html
Kernighan, Brian	http://www.mcs.csuhayward.edu/~morgan/notes_MM6310/MMJava/Chapter_04/K&R.htm
Kertzman, Mitchell	Quote from Softletter, 1/31/97; Biography from http://www.massinc.org/staff/mkertzman.html
Lederberg, Joshua	Biography is at: http://www.almaz.com/nobel/medicine/1958c.html
Liddle, David E.	Biography from http://info.infoseek.com/doc/Reference/Manage.html
Lucky, Robert	Biography is at: http://www.csc.com/csc_vanguard/u_lucky.html
Mandelbrot, Benoit	Biography is at: http://physics.hallym.ac.kr/reference/physicist/Mandelbrot.html
Maritz, Paul, Microsoft	Biography is at: http://www.microsoft.com/corpinfo/staff/paulma.htm; Speech is at: http://www.microsoft.com/BillGates/speeches/sbc/paulmaritz/sbchtm2.htm
Matthews, Max	Biography is at: http://www.xnet.com/~cd/soft.html
McCracken, Edward R.	Biography from www.sgi.com
McGovern, Patrick	Levering, et al, *The Computer Entrepreneurs*, p. 382
McKenna, Regis	Levering, et al, *The Computer Entrepreneurs*, p. 438
McNealy, Scott	Biography from http://www.cspp.org/organize/mcnealy.html; Quote from: *Chief Executive* (U.S.), March 1997, p. 40
Melton, Bill	Biography from http://www.bionomics.org/text/journal/jul96/melton-Biographical information html
Minsky, Marvin	MIT Biography is at: http://alberti.mit.edu/mas/realfac.html; Biography at home page at: http://www.ai.mit.edu/people/minsky/minsky.html; Quote cited at: http://www.pakt.unit.no/~tgs/Quotes/Quotes.htm; see also http://www.ai.mit.edu/people/minsky/papers/sciam.inherit.html
Moore, Gordon	re: Moore's law: http://mason.gmu.edu/~rschalle/moorelaw.html; also: http://research.microsoft.com/research/BARC/Gray/Moore_Law.html
Myhrvold, Nathan	Biography info from http://www.microsoft.com; Quote from ACM97 conference speech, 1997
Negroponte, Nicholas	MIT Biography at: http://alberti.mit.edu/mas/realfac.html
Ozzie, Ray	Quote is from: *Computer Reseller News*, Nov 6 1995, p. 130, see also: http://www.nipltd.com/Main/224e.htm
Palmer, Robert B.	Quote from speech at 1997 *Internet World* conference (http://www.digital.com:80/internet/iworld/palmer.html)

Papert, Seymour	MIT Biography is at: http://alberti.mit.edu/mas/realfac.html; Quote from http://www.pakt.unit.no/~tgs/Quotes/Quotes.htm; see also http://www-mitpress.mit.edu/bookstore/authors/mindstorms.html
Perlman, Steve	Biography from: http://www.webtv.net/corp/HTML/home.steve.html
Platt, Lewis E.	Biography from: http://www.hp.com/abouthp/platt.htm
Poduska, John W., Sr.	Biography from: http://www.avs.com/company/overview/index.htm
Polese, Kim	Biography from http://www.marimba.com
Rashid, Rick	http://www-eecs.mit.edu/AY94-95/events/21.html
Reddy, Raj	Biography from ACM at http://www.acm.org/acm97/conference/perry_reddy.html; see also http://www.ri.cmu.edu/ri-home/rschguide-search.html#Reddy
Ritchie, Dennis	http://www.discovery.com/area/technology/hackers/ritchthomp.html; http://cm.bell-labs.com/who/dmr/; http://cm.bell-labs.com/cm/cs/who/dmr/bigbio1st.html
Rivest, Ronald L.	http://www.certicom.com/html/pks/speakers/rivest.htm; http://www.ns.net/users/payne-o/timeline.html
Robertson, Sandy	Biography from "Legends: Sandy Robertson" by Owen Edwards, *Forbes*, 2/24/97 at http://www.forbes.com/asap/97/0224/112.htm
Rock, Arthur	Levering, et al, *The Computer Entrepreneurs*, p. 454; Quote from: http://connectedpc.com/intel/museum/25anniv/html/int/rock.htm
Saal, Harry J.	Biography notes from: http://www.svi.org/ABOUTSVI/people/hsaal.html
Sanders, Jerry	Biography is at http://www.amd.com/about/history.html; see also: *The Making of Silicon Valley*, The Santa Clara Valley Historical Society
Severino, Paul	Biography notes from: Comtex Newswires: PR Newswire, 06-Jan-1997
Simonyi, Charles	http://mediahistory.com/memory/cm1.html; see also Ralston, *Encyclopedia of Computer Science, Third Edition*, p. 1361 for short discussion of Bravo; http://pcd.stanford.edu/pcd-archives/pcd-fyi/1995/0006.html
Smarr, Larry	Biography is at: Comtex Newswires: US Newswire, Feb 12, 1997; Quote is from: R & D Magazine, Nov 1995, p. 18.
Smith, Alvy Ray	http://wwww.wired.com/wired/4.07/features/microsoft3d.html
Stonebreaker, Michael	*Information Week*, May 13 1996, p. 44
Strecker, Bill	Biography from http://www.decus.org/decus/people/strecker.html; Quote from *DEC Professional*, July 1995, p. 6
Thompson, Ken	http://cm.bell-labs.com/who/ken/; Quote from Lee, p. 662, citing Slater.
Treybig, James	Biography info from http://www.tandem.com/articles/illumina/illumina.htm and Slater, p. 92
Young, John	Biography from http://www.svi.org/ABOUTSVI/people/jyoung.html

Colophon

Wizards and Their Wonders: Portraits in Computing was designed by Gill Fishman Associates in Cambridge, Massachusetts.

The book was designed on Apple Power Macintosh computers and was set in Adobe Garamond, a redesigned version of the classic Garamond font, News Gothic and Franklin Gothic, using Quark Xpress and Adobe Photoshop.

The paper is a 128gsm Japanese Gloss Artpaper.

The book was printed and casebound in China by Lee Fung-Asco.

Gill Fishman Associates

Gill Fishman Associates, Inc. is one of New England's leading corporate design, marketing communications and strategic design firms, providing expertise and consulting in Corporate Identity/Corporate Image programs, Logos, Naming Development, Annual Reports, Web page design and Packaging.

The company is a full-service, creative consulting firm, coordinating the work of writers, editors, printers, photographers and illustrators, and has been honored with over national 100 awards for its work.